What people are saying about *Humanizing Environmental Education* and *201 Nature Activities* by Joel Goodman and Clifford E. Knapp

"Edited by leaders in the field, this is a deeply felt and compelling compendium of some of the forward thinking about the new nature movement and its potential to move our culture forward, not back, to nature."

Richard Louv
Author of Last Child in the Woods, The Nature Principle, and Vitamin N

Joel and Cliff's lifetime work has touched the lives of millions of people. I am delighted that their two new books will continue to make a meaningful, mindful, and heartfelt difference on the planet. These two books are ideal for YMCAs, camps, schools, families, and other settings where we can reach and teach young people and the young at heart about the gifts and blessings of nature and human nature. These books are filled with hundreds of inspiring, intriguing, interesting, insightful, innovative, impactful invitations and activities to help honor Mother Nature and the human spirit at the same time.

Rev. Bruce Tamlyn
Chaplain and Director of Spiritual Life, Silver Bay YMCA

When I first met Joel and Cliff 50 years ago, they were on the ground floor of getting their profound and utterly wise ideas about Environmental Education into the hands of teachers. I was lucky enough to have those two young geniuses as students when I was doing my pioneering work in Values Clarification. I'm so proud to see the gift they have written for you.

Sidney B. Simon, Ed.D.
Professor Emeritus, University of Massachusetts, Amherst
Co-author of Values and Teaching and Values Clarification: A Handbook of Practical Strategies for Teachers and Students

Cliff Knapp's and Joel Goodman's values, vision, passion and working knowledge of nature and human nature are exemplified in these books. Their warm, empathic beliefs in a sense of community and a sense of wonder in the natural world come through clearly. I wholeheartedly recommend these books to you!

Gordon Kaplan
Executive Director (1996 - 2016) American Camp Association, Illinois

"*Humanizing Outdoor and Environmental Education* and *201 Nature and Human Nature Activities* are full of great ideas, examples and reflections on how youth leaders can build appreciation and knowledge of the natural world while at the same time develop self-awareness and interpersonal skills in their participants. This is a gift that young people growing up in the digital age need now more than ever in order to learn the joy and value of balancing screen time indoors with sensory time outdoors."

Donna Ducharme
Chairman, Franklin Grove Creek and Preservation Corporation

As a staff member of a camp based on the writings of Cliff and Joel, I have witnessed the positive impact that this book has had on countless youth from around the country. The abundance of field-tested and classroom-tested activities in these pages has truly enriched so many lives. Joel and Cliff inspire us to treat nature with care and respect and to live with each other in this way as well.

Alan Bartenhagen
Staff, Human Relations Youth Adventure Camp

In this delightful pair of books, Joel and Cliff show that learning is natural: nature has a lot to teach all of us. These two books provide a banquet of thought-provoking insights about the connection between nature and human nature. They are filled with practical, positive, participatory, playful, powerful activities that will engage and enrich the lives of students, campers, adults, and everyone with an interest in living a life connected to the natural world.

> *Dr. Matt Weinstein*
> *Founder and Emperor of Playfair, Inc.*
> *Co-author of Playfair: Everybody's Guide to Noncompetitive Play*

We talk about the growing importance of connecting with nature and connecting with each other. Few books will give you so many wise and wonderful ways of turning this wishful thinking into concrete action – the kinds of action which ensure that however much we upgrade our digital connectivity we do not downgrade our connection with, and enjoyment of, the human and natural world.

> *Dr. Roger Greenaway*
> *Reviewing Skills Training*
> *Stirling, Scotland*

Cliff Knapp and Joel Goodman's two guides blend theory and practice in useful ways. Several chapters provide teachers and group leaders with a rich set of activities to enhance nature awareness and make meaning out of learning experiences. Other chapters present the thinking behind such activities from people like Richard Louv, Cheryl Charles, Joseph Cornell, and Roger Greenaway who have devoted their careers to finding ways to enhance people's connection to the natural world. I will make regular use of these volumes as I plan my own retreats and workshops.

> *Dr. Gregory Smith*
> *Co-editor/co-author of Ecological Education in Action, Place-Based Education in the Global Age, and Place- and Community-Based Education in Schools*

As a former Boy Scout, it's so refreshing to see books that humanize the environment. I mean, that's what we all are—humans in the environment. Joel Goodman and Cliff Knapp have put together a wonderful resource that puts joy and respect into learning about nature. These two books should be part of every young person's education.

> *Ron Culberson, MSW, CSP, CPAE*
> *Speaker, Humorist, and Author of Do it Well, Make it Fun*
> *Past President, National Speakers Association*

As a child participating in Cliff and Joel's programs and later as a young adult staffing them, their educational approach and outdoor activities played a formative role in my personal growth. As an adult working in the field of outdoor education, leading teen wilderness programs and church youth groups, their work mentored my professional development and I applied it to people of all ages and abilities. Any outdoor educator or wilderness guide who needs to expand their range of offerings would serve their clients well by using these books as a guide. Any parents who wish to promote a vital connection to the natural world for their children should carry copies on their family adventures. I am confident that these two books will become as tattered, dog-eared and coffee-stained as mine.

> *John Friauf, LCSW-R*
> *Outdoor Educator, Licensed Guide, School Social Worker*

As our world grows more high tech and as the pace of our lives becomes faster, the need to connect with the natural world and ourselves grows critical. It has become important for educators to find ways to integrate nature and human nature into their curriculum plans. The combination of community building, values clarification, and outdoor adventure is essential and compelling. When you use the ideas in these books, you will witness an amazing transformation of your participants, your staff and even yourself!

Wanda DeWaard
Outdoor Educator and Program Consultant, Earth Kin Programs

Cliff Knapp and Joel Goodman have revised and expanded on the first edition of this valuable experiential learning book. Their work has always been focused on bridging human and natural communities, with special attention to the experience of the learner as an individual and as part of the group. *Humanizing Environmental Education* and *201 Nature and Human Nature Activities* offer educators two timely guides for thinking about and planning authentic experiences that inspire deep learning and commitment.

Dr. David Greenwood
Associate Professor and Canada Research Chair
Department of Environmental Education, Lakehead University, Thunder Bay, Ontario

At a time in history when meaningful personal interaction is overpowered by social media, multi-tasking and an obsession with time-saving, it's refreshing to find a book that celebrates the individual and gently presses us to consider ways to humanize learning. *Humanizing Outdoor and Environmental Education* and its companion *201 Nature and Human Nature Activities* are welcome additions to a societal landscape that often fails to balance content concerns with substantive concern about the well-being of the learner. Thanks to Cliff Knapp and Joel Goodman, we have a tool to restore that balance.

Dr. Herb Broda, Professor Emeritus, Ashland University
Author of Schoolyard-Enhanced Learning and Moving the Classroom Outdoors

For many years I have consulted this guide for inspiration, validation, and important ideas for connecting humans to nature. I know of no other guide that is so easy to use, packed with easily digestible ideas, and stories for bringing humans into the nature equation. When some people focus on the environment, they leave out humans! Big mistake! I am happy to endorse these books and am excited to see the updated versions.

David Stokes
Naturalist, Educator, Entertainer

These books are filled with ideas that guide participants to a holistic understanding of love of others and love of the Earth. The authors recommend that those who teach about the Earth can benefit from those who teach about People. We must strive to truly love one another AND to love the Earth and these books will help create a better world.

Thomas E. Smith, Ph.D.
Clinical Psychologist, Outdoor Therapist, Personal Growth Facilitator

It is time to revive the excitement and creativity of experiential outdoor education! We have widely come to realize the costs of what Richard Louv has called "nature-deficit disorder." Now, more than ever, we as teachers, parents, grandparents, outdoor education staff, and park personnel need to engage our students, children, and park visitors in the kind of experiences in nature that these wonderful books invite us to explore. Ground yourselves in the ideas, principles, and activity ideas these handbooks provide, and get outdoors, in good company, for the joy of it.

Barbara L. Glaser, Ed.D.
Co-Founder, Great Camp Sagamore and Sagamore Institute of the Adirondacks
Regional Commissioner, New York State Dept. of Parks

We suffer because our inaccurate stories separate us from the attractive balance and beauty of Nature in and around us. Happily, *Humanizing Outdoor and Environmental Education* and *201 Nature and Human Nature Activities* provide stories and activities that invite children to visit natural areas where authentic Nature helps them relate with human nature.

> *Michael J. Cohen, Ph.D.*
> *Director, Project NatureConnect*

The survival of civilization depends on the development of an environmental ethic and of behaviors supporting that ethic and a growing concern for a more humanized society. It is imperative that we increase environmental awareness in order to save and protect our planet, our one world. These books show us not just what to do to be connected with our natural world but how to do it while maintaining connections with each other. The character-building, "ageless" activities in these books can be used at home, in the classroom, at nature centers, at camps, adult retreats, and for celebrations of all kinds to gracefully merge both nature awareness and human nature.

> *Beverly Lazar Davis, LCSW-R*
> *Founder, Youth[2]: Youth Helping Youth*
> *Licensed Clinical Social Worker*
> *Past Supervisor, Youth & Family Services Team*

The Rev. Dr. William Sloan Coffin had a way with words: "The world is too dangerous for anything but truth and too small for anything but love." Having led church youth groups for 40 years, the truth is I love these books. This dynamic duo of books will be especially valuable for adult educators, church youth group advisors, and environmental activists. Joel and Cliff have developed a potpourri of practical, step-by-step learning activities leading to an appreciation of nature and the unique gifts every human being has.

> *Rev. Jay Ekman*
> *Retired Pastor, Presbyterian-New England Congregational Church*

These two books are a beautiful blend of the powerful philosophy and practice of humanizing experiential education. The books are loaded with stimulating invitations for people to engage in active and interactive learning. As a coach, I was particularly intrigued and inspired by the grand slam home run chapter on "Creative Leadership: A Humanistic Approach to Coaching"—that was worth the price of admission by itself.

> *Brian Hamm*
> *Amherst College Baseball Head Coach*
> *Winningest Coach in 157 Years*

An understanding of our human relationship to nature has never been more needed than it is today. In native cultures we speak of seven generations, the understanding that what we do now will impact all who follow us for many years to come. Those who will benefit the most from the important teachings in these beautifully written and carefully thought-out books are our children—the ones who truly are the hope for seven generations and more, for a future that extends far beyond fiscal years or presidencies.

> *Joseph Bruchac, Ph.D.*
> *Author of more than 120 books including Keepers of the Earth: Native American*
> *Stories and Environmental Activities for Children*

Joel Goodman and Clifford Knapp are legends in the world of environmental education. Their 1981 book, *Humanizing Environmental Education* is a classic in the field and helped to propel a movement. It is exciting to know that they are again sharing their wisdom and inspiration.

> *Jane Sanborn and Elizabeth Rundle*
> *Co-authors of 101 Nature Activities for Kids*

201 NATURE AND HUMAN NATURE ACTIVITIES

A PRACTICAL GUIDE TO HUMANIZING OUTDOOR AND ENVIRONMENTAL EDUCATION

Joel Goodman
Clifford E. Knapp

ISBN: 978-1-60679-385-5
Library of Congress Control Number: 2017936779
Book layout: Cheery Sugabo
Cover design: Cheery Sugabo
Front cover photo: AlexMax/iStock/Thinkstock
Back cover author photos: Saratoga Photographer (Joel Goodman); Ed Puletz (Clifford E. Knapp)

Healthy Learning
P.O. Box 1828
Monterey, CA 93942
www.healthylearning.com

DEDICATION

This book is dedicated to the people of the communities I have been a part of—family, school, camp, religious, therapeutic, and other human communities where I have touched and been touched. I am especially indebted to Nancy Churchill for her emotional and technical support. There have been so many others in my life who have supported me personally and professionally that space does not permit me to list them here. You know who you are! I am blessed.

—C.E.K.

Cliff and I have been going through labor with twins in creating *201 Nature and Human Nature Activities* and its companion, *Humanizing Outdoor and Environmental Education.* It has been a labor of love. Speaking of which… when we were coming down the homestretch towards giving birth to these two books, my daughter, Alyssa, and her husband, Jake, were also coming down the homestretch of their pregnancy. As we were getting ready for the delivery of "our twins," Alyssa gave birth to Jakobe, Margie's and my first grandchild. He is truly a magical, motivating miracle. Jakobe reminds me of why I do this work: to make the planet healthier and more sustainable for the generations to come. It is with great joy that I dedicate this book to my new-found inspiration, Jakobe.

—J.G.

FOREWORD I:
JACK CANFIELD

When I was a kid, I was a boy scout, went to summer camp, and went on family outings with my brothers and sister and parents. I learned to build a fire without matches, to recognize about fifteen bird calls, to swim across a lake, to row a boat, and to paddle a canoe. Along with my mother I helped nurse birds with broken wings back to health. In the summer I would climb the hills behind our houses in Ohio and West Virginia and hunt for snakes and rabbits. In the winter I would climb to the top of a nearby hill to look for deer or to feed the squirrels that were always there. Nature and the outdoors were very much a part of my life. I felt a kinship with all nature and all forms of life.

The beauty of this book, which Joel Goodman and Cliff Knapp have created, is that it helps us all to reclaim the boundless life that lies dormant within us and so dangerously threatened around us. The book artfully weaves together activities that expand our consciousness of ourselves and of the natural world around us at the same time. The worlds are not as different as they would appear at first glance. Every time I learn to love myself a little bit more, I find that I love all of life a little bit more. Every time I come to a new understanding of the natural processes that abound all around me, I come to more fully understand the natural processes of growth and change that exist within me. The principles are the same—cycles, growth, maturation, decay, rebirth, cooperation, competition, assimilation, integration, and so on. We are of a whole. Whatever affects me affects that which is about me and vice versa.

I have been a classroom teacher, a teacher of teachers, a camp counselor, and a transformational trainer. I found that as a professional aid, this book is more than a gold mine of ideas, new perspectives, and practical methods. It is really six or seven books disguised as one. The book contains more activities than you could ever use in two years of teaching or in a lifetime of camp experiences. I am both amazed and impressed at the depth and breadth of what Joel and Cliff know and share with us in this book.

Whether you are a teacher, camp counselor, wilderness trip facilitator, scout leader, environmental educator, concerned parent, or simply a seeker of the wonder and beauty of the universe and the "youniverse," you are lucky to be reading these words, because as soon as you turn a few more pages, you will have embarked upon a great adventure of healing and wholling yourself and the planet. Have a great trip and enjoy sharing it with others.

—Jack Canfield
Co-creator, #1 *New York Times* best-selling series *Chicken Soup for the Soul*®
Author, *The Success Principles: How to Get From Where You Are to Where You Want to Be*™
www.jackcanfield.com

FOREWORD II:
JOSEPH CORNELL

Dr. Joel Goodman and Dr. Clifford Knapp give us a warm and sensitive approach to environmental learning. Our personal emotions and attitudes powerfully influence the way we view nature, and this is why the really good educator nurtures a sense of well-being in the child. It's as important to get the child to feel good about (and in) nature, as it is to inform him of issues in conservation and ecology.

The authors have been involved in camp and school programs where respect for self and others, trust and caring, cooperation, and a sense of community are explored. Dr. Knapp has described his "secret formula" for these programs like this: "First, I invite the best people I know to join our staff; then campers or students come who want to share outdoor adventure and also to improve their relationships with people. The last step is to give a great deal of energy to helping the group work and play as a community. Fun, learning, and caring just don't appear magically in our lives."

This book shows how Joel Goodman and Cliff Knapp make it work. It will tell you how to teach and encourage: interpersonal rapport, open-mindedness, and curiosity; a sense of values (personal, social, and environmental); feelings of self-worth and confidence; and a community spirit among children and adults alike.

I met Cliff Knapp several times over the years and was impressed by his gentle and sincere nature. I feel that he is an effective communicator for a loving and caring approach to outdoor and environmental education. He and Joel Goodman have written a book that truly "covers all the bases" in humanizing the field. It is thorough, useful, and always puts the child's highest good—body, mind, and soul—first. I feel that the book will play an important role in helping us to lovingly encourage the child's awareness of and enthusiasm for nature and human nature.

—Joseph Cornell
Founder and President, Sharing Nature Worldwide
Nature Awareness Educator and Author

CONTENTS

    #1: Limiting Senses

    #2: Expanding Senses

    #3: Quest for Questions

    #4: Role Playing and Using Metaphors

    #5: Guide Sheets, Scavenger Hunts, and Factual Information

    #6: Question Trail

    #7: Naming Trail

    #8: Awareness Theme Cards

    #9: Environmental Task Cards

    #10: Nature's Band

    #11: Tree Fantasy

    #12: Recalling Highpoints Outdoors

    #13: Pretending

    #14: Body Twisting

    #15: Analysis of Characteristics

    #16: Changing Characteristics

    #17: Compare and Contrast

    #18: New Uses

    #19: Autobiography

    #20: Sense Probe

    #21: Figures of Speech

    #22: Assigning Numbers

    #23: If I Had…

    #24: Jigsaw Puzzle

    #25: Environmental Factors

    #26: Opposite Lines

    #27: Shopping Center Search

COMING TO TERMS WITH THE TRIP

Throughout our two companion books (*Humanizing Outdoor and Environmental Education* and *201 Nature and Human Nature Activities*), the masculine shall be deemed to include the feminine and vice versa.

There are several terms used throughout the two books that need further explanation. In describing students in a classroom, campers, members of a family, people in an organization, and athletes on a team, we use the word "participants." In speaking of teachers, naturalists, camp leaders and counselors, parents, coaches, and other helping professionals who might use the activity ideas in this book, we use the word "staff" or "leader." In talking about planned and structured activities for a classroom, nature center, outdoor school, camp, family, recreation center, and other arenas in which outdoor and environmental education could take place, we use the word "program" or "curriculum." As you read this book, please make your own personal translations when you come across any of these words.

As you'll see, we have presented a wealth of strategies that invite active participation and learning in these two books. In some activities, the directions are given to the staff. In other activities, they are stated as if given directly to the participants. In all activities, our first mantra is "Safety first!" With awareness of your group's abilities and limitations, we encourage you to use your creativity and good judgment in implementing or adapting the activities to maximize both safety and learning.

CHAPTER 1
WELCOME TO THE HUMANIZING TRIANGLE

gpointstudio/iStock/Thinkstock

"Once we realize that the nature within and the nature without are continuous, then we too may share and manifest the exquisite beauty and effortless grace associated with the natural world."

—John Seed

Welcome to an eye-opening, mind-opening, practical guide to planning and leading nature and human nature activities in classrooms, camps, outdoor and environmental education programs, YMCAs, Boys Clubs and Girls Clubs, parks, recreation programs, sports teams, and families. This book springboards off our companion book, *Humanizing Outdoor and Environmental Education* (see the Resources chapter) and presents you with a plethora of 201 pragmatic, positive, playful, powerful, people-and-planet-pleasing possibilities.

This book is based on three core ideas, each represented by the sides of a triangle. All three sides are needed to form the shape and provide the strength for humanizing outdoor and environmental programs and curricula. One side of the triangle represents *intrapersonal*—the self-knowledge skills that help access our feeling lives, such as our self-concept and values. Another represents *interpersonal*—the human community-building skills needed to read the intentions and desires of others for getting along, working, and living with them. The third side of the triangle is *extrapersonal* and represents our *mindfulness of nature* and its natural wonders. This sensitivity to the Earth is not only important for the gifts it gives to maintain our emotional well-being, but also for our physical survival on the planet. All three sides of this Humanizing Triangle provide the foundation for the 201 activities found in this book.

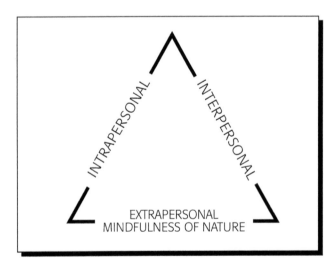

A long list of practical activities is not enough for leaders to implement quality programs or curricula in a variety of settings. Leaders who are equipped with well-thought-out educational philosophies, people skills, and a laundry list of quality activities can succeed in making the world a more peaceful and humane place… and may even be a step towards helping to preserve and protect our planet in the process.

The outdoors is an unlimited source of inspiration and rich context for learning about others and us. Nature can be a mirror for seeing and comprehending human nature. Millions of people gather each year all over the world to learn about themselves and their communities, as they experience the plants, animals, mountains, oceans, streams, stars, soil, and air. Mother Nature can become a teacher, if we pay attention to the lessons and understand the languages she speaks.

Some people may believe that self-understanding, improved human relations skills, and saving the planet are worthy goals, but that they are difficult to accomplish. They think that because the goal is complex, it is impossible. They don't realize that by simply adding an apostrophe to the word "Impossible", it can be changed to "I'm possible!"

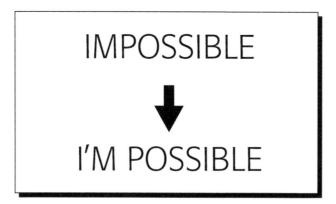

1+1 > 2: PUTTING HUMANISTIC EDUCATION TOGETHER WITH OUTDOOR AND ENVIRONMENTAL EDUCATION

The possibilities are endless, when we bring together humanistic education and outdoor/environmental education. The whole is definitely greater than the sum of the parts, when we synthesize humanistic and outdoor/environmental education. This book is overflowing with nature and human nature activities that:

- consider the human relations component of teaching about the environment
- honor the close interaction between nature and human nature
- teach about nature awareness, communication, community building, valuing, and self-esteem outdoors
- establish a better balance between screen time indoors and sensory time outdoors
- respond to the societal need for a more holistic connection with the natural world
- celebrate a sense of wonder and a sense of place in nature and human nature
- guide natural teachers and other youth leaders with creative ideas for teaching about our fragile planet
- speak to the societal threat of becoming an apathetic bystander to impending environmental challenges

- increase our empathy and reverence for all living things and the Earth
- respect our indigenous past and gentle ways of walking on the planet

Outdoor and environmental education put *nature* back in education. Humanistic education puts *human nature* back in education. This book is a synthesis of nature and human nature educational activities that link people with our planet. Some of the activities take place indoors … some in the great outdoors. Some are individual mindfulness or reflection opportunities. Some are pair, small-group, and large-group exercises. There are many different delightful flavors of activities awaiting you. Before plunging in, we would like to give you a quick sense of "where we're coming from." (For a more detailed look, our companion book, *Humanizing Outdoor and Environmental Education* is a thought-full guide to leading nature and human nature activities and provides an in-depth foundation for *201 Nature and Human Nature Activities*.)

HUMANISTIC EDUCATION: THIS WE BELIEVE

Both authors have developed educational philosophies that guide our selection of structured activities when we facilitate groups. We share with you the following dozen as food for thought: 12 beliefs about designing and implementing programs and curricula when leading others in *humanizing outdoor and environmental education*. We believe that people:
- Share a desire for recognition, caring, acceptance, self-esteem, identity, security, challenge, freedom, fun, and intellectual and emotional growth.
- Have inner wisdom about what they value and want help in clarifying the values they are unsure of as they strive to achieve their life goals.
- Hope to be part of a positive, supportive, affirming learning environment where bullying, negativity, and put-downs are out-of-bounds.
- Want to become more aware of themselves and others by reflecting on their own thoughts and feelings and listening to the thoughts and feelings of others.
- Value interpersonal cooperation in reaching their personal goals as well as *intrapersonal* competition in their search to improve themselves.
- Find satisfaction in accomplishing personal and group goals that they have had opportunities to co-create.
- Want to assume more responsibility for their own self-direction, self-discipline, and self-evaluation as they mature.
- Respond best to situations in which their uniqueness and special attributes are recognized and nurtured.
- Have varying requirements for being alone for contemplation and being with others for socialization.
- Have the potential for creative problem-solving, conflict resolution, and decision-making, if given opportunities and supportive conditions.

- Want their leaders to create a learning environment filled with support, empathy, genuineness, honesty, trust, respect, and passion for the subject at hand.
- Want their learning experience to be fun, but not for fun. They want learning and laughing to go hand-in-hand, as participants experience meaningful educational opportunities. You will find many activities in this collection that are learning-filled and laughter-fueled. There is a connection between AHA! and HAHA!

SELECTING CRITERIA FOR A HUMANIZING ACTIVITY

With the 201 activities in this book, you will be facing a large banquet table. How do you decide on which activities to taste? Which ones will be your appetizers? Your main course? Your dessert?

What follows is some more food for thought for you—some questions you can ask yourself to help you get started on your fun feast. You can tap your creativity to add to the 201 activities and generate your own humanizing activities by considering these criteria as guidelines. These criteria can also double as evaluation principles. Of course, any one activity may not meet all of the criteria—hopefully, you could put together a "recipe" for your program that would be well balanced in terms of the following:

- Does the activity speak to one or more of your broad program goals?
- Does the activity seem to be consistent with your organizing principles?
- Given the particular focus of your program, does the activity fit?
- Does the activity provide opportunities for learning new skills (e.g., such life skills as communicating, community-building, decision-making, etc.)?
- Does the activity encourage cooperation and group cohesiveness?
- Does the activity primarily use the natural setting and local areas and people?
- Does the activity enhance self-esteem and feelings of success?
- Does the activity introduce a sense of fun and adventure?
- Does the activity encourage creative outlets for energy?
- Does the activity invite participation and involvement?
- Does the activity consider the environment (i.e., does not harm a quality environment)?
- Does the activity accommodate for individual differences in ability and preferences?
- Does the activity consider the health and safety of the participants?
- Does the activity provide opportunities for the participants to make choices—does the activity offer "structured freedom"?
- Does the activity speak to the needs, interests, and readiness level of the participants?
- Does the activity flow in a way that is logically and psychologically sound (e.g., moving from lower risk to higher risk; moving from introduction of a new skill to planned reinforcement of that skill)?
- Does the activity include variety (e.g., of groupings; of learning/teaching modes; a balance between seriousness and lightness; energizers and changes of pace)?

- Does the activity include opportunities for self-evaluation, for reflection, for "processing" or making sense/meaning of the activity?
- Does the activity have follow-up (i.e., do participants know how to springboard off the activity)?
- Does the activity include the following steps: (A) attending (have you built in an initial attention-grabber?); (B) experiencing (have you included opportunities for participants to be actively involved?); (C) conceptualizing (have you provided time for the participants to "make sense" of their experience?); (D) relating (have you given the participants a chance to relate what they have learned to their own lives and values?); (E) practicing (have you invited participants to "try out" and apply their learning to their own lives?).

Can you think of other criteria that would be important for you to consider in generating and sequencing your program's activities? Take some time to create your own list (or add to the aforementioned list). This step is crucial if you are to go beyond merely following "recipes" for activities. Ultimately, we need to have more cooks, not only more cookbooks.

ANATOMY OF AN OUTDOOR/ENVIRONMENTAL EDUCATION EXPERIENCE

When conducting an outdoor/environmental education experience, leaders must consider many variables during the design process, including the following:
- How can you, as leader, help establish a positive rapport and supportive learning community climate?
- Do the participants feel cared for and comfortable in this place?
- Who is the designated leader(s)? What is her experience in this role?
- Who are the participants/leaders assembled here?
- Do they know each other already or are they mostly strangers? If not, what happens?
- Do you, as leader, have the proper attire and equipment for today?
- What are the intended goals and objectives for this experience?
- What are the agenda and time allotments for this experience?
- How important is it to honor this plan?
- Are you flexible to allow for new spontaneous and/or co-created activities?
- What are the ground rules, group norms, or guidelines?
- What expectations do the participants have for this experience?
- What feedback will the participants give to help you, as leader, become more effective?
- How often will you, as leader, request group feedback about the experience?
- What outdoor activity will you begin with?
- Were clear directions given so everyone understands what to do? How do you know?
- Why are you doing this? (What is the purpose of the activity?)

- How long might it take to complete?
- What are the boundaries for movements in this area?
- How will you know when to re-assemble?
- Will this be an individual, small-group, or total-group activity?
- Will there be reports to the whole group when the activity is finished?
- Will the experience be reviewed, processed, or reflected upon? If so, when?
- What strategies will be suggested for reviewing/processing this experience?
- What aspects of the experience will be examined (group dynamics, knowledge [concepts, skills, attitudes, values, habits of mind], feelings/emotions)?
- How will you know when it is time to move on to the next planned activity?
- What will the next activity be? Does it make sense to do this one next?
- How often and how long will rest/relaxation breaks be?
- How many activities should be planned for each session?
- When is it time to end?
- What kind of ending will be most effective?
- Is there a need to stay in communication with the group? If so, how will this be done?
- Is there time for questions and answers or to plan for the next session?
- What other important questions were not included in this list of variables?

READY ... SET ... GO!

Now that you probably have met your quota of *questions*, let's get going on your *quest* for 201 field-tested, classroom-tested, engaging, enjoyable, entertaining, educational exercises exploring nature and human nature. On your mark ... get set ... grow!

> *"We need to send into space a flurry of artists and naturalists, photographers and painters, who will turn the mirror upon ourselves and show us Earth as a single planet, a single organism that's buoyant, fragile, blooming, buzzing, full of spectacles, full of fascinating human beings, something to cherish."*
>
> —Diane Ackerman

CHAPTER 2

MINDFULNESS AND COMING TO YOUR SENSES: ENVIRONMENTAL AND PEOPLE AWARENESS

paulaphoto/iStock/Thinkstock

"Everyone has many associations with a flower. You put out your hand to touch it, or lean forward to smell it, or maybe touch it with your lips almost without thinking, or give it to someone to please them. But one rarely takes the time to really see a flower."

—Georgia O'Keefe

Buckminster Fuller once defined the word "environment" as "everything except me." Using this definition, you can consider the environment to include things, such as trees, rocks, water, soil, sunlight, and the surrounding people. The big problem of drawing strict lines between people and their environment is that we might overlook our close interdependence on and interrelationship with our surroundings. We must keep in mind Wendell Berry's words: "The earth is what we all have in common, it is what we are made of and what we live from, and we cannot damage it without damaging those with whom we share it." Activities that combine awareness and mindfulness of both nature and people are excellent vehicles for humanizing programs and curricula. The activities in this chapter are designed with this two-fold purpose in mind.

The words "awareness" and "mindfulness" are used freely and often broadly in writings today. Awareness occurs when you combine the sensory input from the outer environment with thoughts and feelings from the inner environment (yourself) to produce meaning. Mindfulness is being present in the moment and paying attention to what you are experiencing. You should keep a soft and open mind to concentrate and see things as they are without judgment. If you were to view the planet with this kind of openness and readiness, you would find wisdom.

To make a personal connection with the environment, certain conditions must be present, including the following:

- physical comfort (awareness is stifled when a person is too cold, wet, or tired)
- open or receptive attitude (unless a person wants awareness, no awareness will occur)
- sensory intake (one or more of the senses must be functioning in order for a person to reach a level of awareness); and
- environmental stimuli (the environment must provide the stimuli in order for awareness to result).

There are several "hooks" (refer to the first five listed activities in this chapter) that help create the conditions that invite a person to develop awareness and mindfulness. This chapter features 35 activities to help you practice what we teach.

ACTIVITIES

❑ Activity #1: Limiting Senses

At first, the technique of limiting senses appears to be counter to one of the prerequisites for awareness. However, by limiting one or more senses, the others are often heightened. The blindfold, which is often used in this type of activity, enables the senses of hearing, touch, or smell to be heightened. Other methods of limiting senses can involve taping the thumbs to the palm, putting gloves on before trying to identify textures, or not talking for a period of time. The limiting-senses technique also serves to provide a person with greater appreciation for the limited sense, once it is freed for use again.

❑ Activity #2: Expanding Senses

This technique does exactly what is described—it extends or focuses the senses through the use of a sensory aid or gimmick. These techniques can involve gadgets, such as toilet tissue rolls, used as "cameras;" cardboard frames to narrow and focus the field of vision; "task cards" to focus attention on something, using words; cupping hands behind the ears to gather in more sound, or merely repeating such words as "Now I am aware that …" or "I wonder if …"

❑ Activity #3: Quest for Questions

The time-honored question can serve as an awareness hook. Open-ended questions often serve as effective ways of capturing attention. Sometimes, the more ambiguous and unspecific the question is, the more the participant can supply the missing parts and arrive at more creative answers. So often, the answers to questions far exceed the expectations of the leader and provide more environmental awareness for the whole group. We believe that asking a good question sometimes expands awareness more than giving facts about what is observed.

❑ Activity #4: Role-Playing and Using Metaphors

One method of producing creative thinking is to "make the strange familiar and the familiar strange." In other words, by examining the environment in new and different ways, awareness can result. By playing the role of an earthworm, for example, you are forced to see the world in a new way. The simile, a way of comparing two apparently unrelated things, using the words "like" or "as," is another way to encourage awareness. For example, to see a snake like a "painted and textured rope" may help you see the beautiful patterns of the scales. Allegories and analogies will accomplish similar purposes.

❑ Activity #5: Guide Sheets, Scavenger Hunts, and Factual Information

Not to be discounted are the guided-discovery techniques, similar to those used in nature trail booklets or scavenger hunts. If a person is motivated to learn about the environment, guided directives or inspiring quotations can invite new awareness. For example, the direction to "lift the fallen log to see what you can find underneath" can help expand a participant's world. Also, facts, such as "the sassafras has three distinctly different shaped leaves," can stimulate investigation. Invitations to find, count, measure, or estimate can also open up new awareness. Distributing quotations along the trail can encourage discovery of awareness. For example, "Each part of nature teaches that the passing away of one life is the making room for another" (Henry David Thoreau). Find evidence of a passing away of life.

❑ Activity #6: Question Trail

Prior to introducing the Question Trail activity, go outside and put numbered stakes, baggage tags, or pieces of cardboard at designated locations. These numbered locations will become "stations" or stops along a Question Trail.

This activity is called "Question Trail" because instead of factual information given at each station, one or more questions is asked. Each question invites some type of exploration and results in a new awareness at that location. Initially, small groups of three or four persons are assigned to each station and told to compile a list of questions about that spot. After each group has compiled questions, the whole group is led to each successive number and invited to answer the questions. This activity provides for a success experience for most people while asking and answering the questions. This activity also gets people away from the erroneous idea that they must be able to identify a plant, rock, or animal by name in order to learn something about it.

For example, when a group is examining a decaying stump, the following questions could be asked: Can you find any living things using the stump for an apartment?; Does the rotten wood hold water like a sponge? How is this stump like a person you know? How many words can you find to describe this stump to a friend who is blind? How many colors can you find on the stump?; and Of what kind of animal does the stump remind you?

❑ Activity #7: Naming Trail

Select a location outside where two types of environments join (for example, where a field joins a forest, a vacant lot joins a sidewalk, water joins a bank, or a road joins a field). Usually, the area where two ecosystems meet will provide a greater variety of plant and animal life. Ask the participants to each take 10 toothpicks or small sticks and 10 small slips of paper and use them to mark numbered stations along a section of the edge trail.

The object of this activity is to name the plant or animal evidence by making up names that are based on its characteristics. No real common names should be used even if they are known. For example, a toothpick and paper numbered with a "1" can be placed next to a dandelion and called "fuzzy head," after the cottony seed head. The same plant could be named "garden hose plant," after the flexible, hollow stem supporting the flower or seed head. Next, a toothpick with a piece of paper numbered "2" could be placed next to a clover leaf. This plant could be named "triple leaf," after the three-part leaf. After each participant has named 10 plants or animal evidence, they pair up to share their trails. This activity stresses awareness of characteristics and creativity in assigning a name, based on these characteristics. This technique also illustrates how many plants and animals are named for obvious physical characteristics.

❑ Activity #8: Awareness Theme Cards

Prepare a deck of 3 x 5 cards beforehand on which a theme word or words are written, one to a card. Among the words that can help direct awareness in the environment are the following: decay, lifecycles, bark, moisture, coolness, weeds, seeds, roots, animal food, insect evidence, protective covering, arts and crafts, plants, fences, water, manhole covers, gutters, telephone wires, motion, patterns, cooperation, textures, waste, cruelty, variety, symmetry, harmony, and repetition. Many more awareness themes can be added to explore a particular area. The human interaction is increased, if teams of two or three participants are assigned to find evidence in the environment of the theme written on each card.

Another way to use theme cards is to prepare different roles people can play, as they walk along the trail. Increase the fun by having the group guess what role each person is playing. Examples of such roles include the following: toucher, lifter, looker up, looker down, doubter, questioner, exclaimer, listener, smeller, and searcher.

❑ Activity #9: Environmental Task Cards

Environmental task cards direct participants to explore their surroundings. Typically, the tasks are worded briefly and allow a variety of interpretations and responses. Usually, boundaries of time and location are established and participants go alone or choose a partner to explore each card. The tasks may be completed by bringing objects back, sketching them, or verbally describing them.

The sharing session following the completion of the tasks is just as important as the discovery part. Participants should be encouraged to select task cards, even if the solutions are not clear before beginning. Some of the tasks are ambiguous to force participants to make decisions and be creative. Participants are to do the task in any way they feel is best. Guidelines should be provided about not picking plants that are threatened, poisonous, or on the property of others. It is important to maintain a nonjudgmental and accepting atmosphere throughout the sharing of the results after completing the tasks. Participants may wish to "pass," if the sharing is considered too personal. Examples of task cards include the following:

- Go outside and stand in a spot that is as near to sea level as possible. Prove to someone else that you are at the lowest elevation around. How long would it take you to reach sea level?
- Go outside and find pebbles to create a rock rainbow. How many colors are in your rock rainbow? Crush some soft rocks and mix them with water or glue to make "face paint."
- Find a collage that was not made by people. Duplicate a natural collage. Rearrange the elements of a natural collage. Add to a natural collage.
- Make a list of changes that occur, while you watch some things outside. How many can you list in five minutes? Which changes are not reversible?
- Look under two things, inside of three things, around four things, and through five things. What other ways can you look at things in your environment? Look in those ways. What in the environment is not a thing? How can you examine a non-thing?
- Go outside and find plants or plant parts that resemble or remind you of other things. Make sketches of the parts and next to each write what it resembles or reminds you of. Find parts of plants that remind you of body parts (both inside and outside of you). Using plant parts, make something beautiful, useful, ugly, or scary. Try to become a particular plant or plant part. What happened to you when you did?

- Go outside and ask a question, make a hypothesis about the answer, and design an experiment to test that hypothesis.
- Go outside and crush parts of abundant plants to smell the aroma of each. Which smell would make a good deodorant or perfume?
- Go outside and find the home of some living thing that you would most enjoy living in. Describe a house you know that has one feature of this animal home. How would you like to change your home so it is more like this animal's home? How is your present home not like this animal's home?
- Go outside and find small objects that resemble squares, ellipses, circles, triangles, diamonds, and rectangles. Group these objects into different categories according to color, texture, living and dead, light and heavy. Make up other categories to group them in those ways. Name three ways that all the objects are similar. Which ones were there because of people? If you were to make animals out of these objects, what animals would you make? Pick one object and use your senses in as many ways as possible to learn more about it.
- Go outside and find an insect. Mark the spot where you find it. Follow it for five minutes. How far did you travel? Try to retrace your steps. What do you admire about that insect? Give your insect a name and talk to it for a while. What would the insect say to you, if it could talk? If you could choose one kind of insect to be your friend, which would it be? How is a particular insect like you?
- Go outside and make a list of rules that people have made that have affected or changed the environment. Which rules are not necessary? What evidence can you find of natural rules? Can you find examples of natural rules and people-made rules in conflict with each other?
- Go outside and look up. What do you see that you haven't noticed before? What is the color of the sky? How does this color change? Find some clouds in the sky. Are they moving? Pick a tiny wisp of cloud and follow it for a few minutes. Does it disappear or build in size? Find familiar shapes in the clouds. What can you learn from looking down?
- Go outside and select an object that can be found in abundance (e.g., acorns, fallen leaves, sand grains, pebbles, or sticks). What is the most of any one object that you can carry in one hand? Can you hold twice as many objects in two hands? What tool could you invent to hold more objects in one hand? Invent the tool and see how many objects you can hold.
- Go outside and pick an area where you would like to spend some time alone. How much time would you like to spend there? What characteristics of that spot influenced your decision? Find an area that is completely different from the one you picked first. Would you like to spend some time there, too? How much? What are some of your thoughts and feelings while spending time in that spot?
- Go outside and find a color that represents the following feelings: sad, glad, mad, and scared. How many mood colors did you find? Does the color of something in the environment affect your feelings toward the object?

- Go outside and find something that is dead. Write or deliver a eulogy, giving praise for its accomplishments. Try to figure out the following: cause and time of death, names and numbers of survivors, how the object will be missed on earth, and other important information about the departed one. How is death valuable to the environment?
- Go outside and listen to some moving water in a brook, gutter, drain, lake, or reservoir. Can you hear sounds that resemble words in the English language? Don't give up too soon; you may hear the moving water "speak." Does a brook really babble?

❏ Activity #10: Nature's Band

Give the participants instructions to go into the environment and find objects that can be used to create some music. Objects, such as sticks, stones, leaves, husks, pods, seeds, metal pipes, car brake drums, garbage can lids, and bottles, as well as many other objects, can produce tone and rhythm. Conduct a musical "happening" in which instruments join together one by one and blend into an unrehearsed composition. A musical piece can be written by assigning each instrument a line on a grid written on a piece of newsprint. Each time the instrument is to be played, an "x" is placed along the grid horizontally. The conductor moves a baton along the grid horizontally to signal the instruments to be played. Nature's band creates a group effort, which tends to expand awareness of nature and the people-made environment, as well as results in feelings of teamwork and cooperation among the band members.

❏ Activity #11: Tree Fantasy

Ask the participants to select a tree from the surrounding area. The participants then assume a comfortable position and close their eyes. The leader conducts a slow-moving fantasy in which the participants pretend that they are small enough to travel inside of that tree. The guided journey can begin by entering the tree through a small hole in the leaf. The inside of the leaf is explored and then the branches, trunk, and roots. With the imagination of the leader and participants, an exciting journey can be conducted. After the journey, the participants can share their feelings about exploring the inside of a tree throughout the seasons. The sharing phase of this activity is just as important as the fantasy journey. The leader can learn about how fluids and nutrients move in a tree through various vessels to make the fantasy more real.

❏ Activity #12: Recalling Highpoints Outdoors

The participants assume a comfortable position and close their eyes. The leader conducts a guided tour of past experiences and memories in the outdoors. The purpose of this activity is to relax and recall positive, past associations with the environment. It is important to dwell upon positive experiences in order to accomplish the purpose of relaxation and refreshment. The participants are advised to only think of happy or pleasant experiences that are triggered by the leader's words. You may select words from the following list or make up new ones. Mention them slowly to provide time to savor each one:

Joel Goodman

The silent flutter of a butterfly, the smell of a beautiful flower, the sight of a stream in the mountains, sawdust in a woodshop, freshly cut grass, the sound of crickets chirping, the smell of a campfire, wet sand between the toes, sunshine warmth on a cool day, the taste of a freshly picked apple, walking through leaves in the fall, the smell and feel of pine needles on the ground, the sound of a bird in the early morning, a sunset over a lake, a gentle breeze accompanied by the salty smell of the ocean, and on and on.

It is important to provide opportunities for the participants to share their thoughts and feelings after the experience if they wish.

❑ Activity #13: Pretending

Examine your environment from different points of view by role-playing various types of people or pretending you are a plant, animal, or object. Allow your imagination to run wild. For example, look at a utility pole as if you were: a creature from another planet; a telephone repair worker; or a child flying a kite nearby. Pretend to be a plant, animal, or object looking at a utility pole, such as some grass growing at the base; a hungry termite; or a telephone cable.

❑ Activity #14: Body Twisting

Examine the environment by adjusting your body position, moving, or doing something different with your body. For example, how would a utility pole look while lying flat on your back beneath it? How would it look from on top of a stepladder? How would it look while standing on your head or lying on your side? How would it look while hopping up and down on one foot? How would it look while squinting your eyes? How would it look from a helicopter?

❑ Activity #15: Analysis of Characteristics

Examine the environment to determine how each characteristic of an object is related to the function. For example:

- Characteristic—height of a utility pole and its relation to function: the height of the pole enables the cable to be suspended above the street for safety.
- Characteristic—straightness and its relation to function: the straightness makes the pole easier to pile, transport, and to erect.
- Characteristic—dark-colored wood and its relation to function: the dark wood preservative slows decay and insect damage, so the pole will last longer.

Among the other characteristics you may want to examine are color, size (height and width), composition, location (surrounding objects), shape, decorations or symbols, hardness, sound (or sound when tapped), smell, taste (use caution in tasting some substances), texture, pattern, or movement.

❏ Activity #16: Changing Characteristics

Examine the characteristics of an object to see how each one could be changed so that the object would serve its function better. For example, utility poles can be: made of clear plastic so they will be less visible to those who think they are an eyesore; made of metal so they won't decay as fast as wood; and be erected farther apart so that fewer poles are needed along scenic highways.

❏ Activity #17: Compare and Contrast

Compare and contrast characteristics of an object to those of other objects of the same type. For example, how does the height of this pole compare with other poles I've seen? How does the color of the wood compare with other poles I've seen? How do the symbols (abbreviations, words, and numbers) compare with those on other poles?

Activities #18-25 that follow use a utility pole as an example. Any other human-made or natural object may be substituted.

❏ Activity #18: New Uses

Examine the object to see how it could be used in new ways. For example, a utility pole can be used as: a unit of length to measure heights of surrounding buildings, trees, and other objects; a place to post signs and erect billboards; or a place to erect birdhouses and feeders to increase bird populations.

❏ Activity #19: Autobiography

Write an autobiography about an object, as though you were that object. Include where you came from, how you got here, how long you have been there, how long you will be there, why you were put there, who visits you, how you change, and how you are important to people and the environment. The following provides an example of the activity in practice:

> *"Before I was cut, I was a tree growing in the south. I was a southern pine and chosen because I was straight and tall and at least eight*

inches in diameter. I was transported first by train and then by truck to where I was treated with a preservative called penta. I was purchased by the local telephone company, which erected me last year because the previous pole was decayed and weak. Occasionally, a bird sits on top of me, and the sun and rain have caused me to be a lighter color in places ..."

❑ Activity #20: Sense Probe

Use your senses to learn new things about an object. When you discover some new things about it, use this information to describe the object to someone who has never seen it before. For example:

- *Sight:* With a magnifying lens, examine the wood of the utility pole. Step back from the pole and stare at it carefully. Then, look behind the object, without moving behind it.

- *Hearing:* Does the utility pole make sounds as the wind passes by the wires? Cup your hands behind your ears and face the pole. Does this help you hear better? Tap the area around your ear gently to sensitize it to hearing small sounds. Then, tap the pole in different places to determine if it makes different sounds. Describe the sounds you hear from the pole, either using words (whirr, buzz, etc.) or make visual sketches of the sound.

- *Touch:* Use your cheek, nose, arm, or foot to touch the pole, as well as your fingers. Which part of your body helps you become aware of something new? Make rubbings of the symbols or wood texture by placing a piece of paper over it and rubbing with a crayon or soft lead pencil.

- *Taste:* Taste is a more difficult sense to use with the pole because of dangers of poisonous materials. Exercise extreme caution in tasting experiments and warn the participants against indiscriminate tasting of plants, animals, and chemicals. A number of substances exist, however, that can be tasted in order to learn more about the environment.

- *Smell:* Smell the utility pole. What is the strongest odor that you smell? Does it smell the same all over? Compare the smells to familiar materials.

❑ Activity #21: Figures of Speech

Use analogies, metaphors, similes, personification, onomatopoeia, and allegories to enable participants to gain new perspectives of objects. Examples of this activity include the following: telephone lines are the veins and arteries of the telephone's body; telephone poles hike over mountains and through valleys, carrying important messages on their backs; telephone poles are trees stripped of their arms and clothing and replanted again; telephone poles are like city fence posts; and the wind whipping the lines makes a swishing, buzzing sound.

❏ Activity #22: Assigning Numbers

Examine an object and think of as many ways as possible to assign numbers to it. For example, how much did the pole cost the telephone company? How tall is the pole? What is its diameter and circumference? How much does it weigh?

❏ Activity #23: If I Had …

Imagine that you have superhuman powers, such as x-ray eyes, long-distance vision, magnifying eyes, super-powered hearing, very sensitive touch and smell, or immunity to any poisonous chemicals. Using these imaginary powers, ask the question, "If I had _____, how would I perceive this object differently?" For example, if I had x-ray eyes, I could see inside the pole to count the growth rings to find out how old the tree was when it was cut; and if I had long-distance vision, I could see all the poles in my state to find out how many there are.

❏ Activity #24: Jigsaw Puzzle

Using your imagination, take an object apart and put the pieces back together again (all in your mind). For example:

> When I start to detach the wires on the utility pole, I notice wires of different thicknesses. The thin ones are the electric wires, and the thicker ones are the telephone wires. The thinner ones lead to a large container (transformer). Some wires are attached directly to the pole, while others are connected to shiny, odd-shaped things (insulators). I need to tear off a wire that is attached along the full length of the pole and runs into the ground (ground wire). It will be difficult to take off. (During the process of taking the utility pole apart, new discoveries may raise other questions, leading to a greater awareness of the pole and its function.)

❏ Activity #25: Environmental Factors

Determine how different environmental factors affect an object. These factors can include: sunlight, precipitation, humidity, wind, heat, cold, animals (including humans), plants, and other forces that change and affect objects in the environment. The following examples illustrate the activity: rain causes some of the wood preservative to wash away; sunlight causes some of the preservative to become sticky and some other areas to fade in color; and the repairman puts spike holes in the pole, when he climbs it with special boots.

❏ Activity #26: Opposite Lines

Using the following lines, inventory the environment by placing the names of objects and events in position on each line. For example:

Hot _____	Cold
Fast _____	Slow
Light _____	Dark
High _____	Low
Loud _____	Soft
Straight _____	Curved
Old _____	New
Quiet _____	Noisy
Good _____	Bad
Cooperative _____	Competitive
Moving _____	Still

❏ Activity #27: Shopping Center Search

In looking at the human-made environment, investigate a shopping center to answer the following questions: How many cars will the parking lot hold? Is there evidence of traffic congestion? How much water is used each week and how is it used? How is the center lighted at night? How much does it cost? How is the merchandise received and distributed throughout the shopping center? What types of refuse accumulate and how is it disposed? What changes could be made in the shopping center environment to attract more shoppers? What are some reasons that customers give for shopping there? Is there any cooperation between individual merchants in the shopping center with regard to refuse disposal, litter cleanup, window washing, or theft protection? What type of communications system is established within the shopping center? How have the building and parking lot affected the water drainage patterns in the area? What types of safety hazards can be located? What kinds of conveniences and services are available to the customers (restrooms, drinking fountains, diaper-changing places, and benches)? What negative consequences on the natural environment might there be from the shopping center?

❏ Activity #28: The Art of Seeing a City Block

This activity invites you to be creative in how you perceive a familiar environment (e.g., your own block or neighborhood). Generate a series of questions that encourage new perspectives, and then act as a "tour guide" for others. The following is an example of a tour arranged for a block in Saratoga Springs, New York:

- Exit this building on Spring Street—go west, young person. Look very carefully at this old building. Is the brickwork uniform throughout? What might account for this?

- Go to the utility pole marked as follows:

  Koppers

  CH–70

  SP–P

  5–40

- What do you think these codes mean? What other characteristics reveal the story of this pole?
- Continue across the street and observe the other church building. What do the two dates mean on the cornerstone?
- Look up toward the roof. What animal evidence can you find?
- What kind of plant is growing near the roof?
- Now look down to see how many different kinds of plants are growing along the base of the building and between the sidewalk cracks. Sketch one plant that you recognize.
- How is this building currently being used?
- Look for a four-leaved clover next to the sidewalk. What good luck has entered your life recently?
- If a raindrop fell in the center of the street, where would it roll? Pretend that you are a raindrop and see where you flow.
- Notice the evergreen in front of the Skidmore Shop. Look at the underside of a needle. Can you find the "railroad track" markings?
- Along the way, smile and greet any people you meet. What are their reactions?
- Stop for a moment at the corner of Spring and Circular Streets. What would you do if you discovered a fire in one of the buildings nearby? In what direction would you go to find a hospital for the injured?
- Examine the old lamppost on the corner. Can you find others within sight?
- Head south on Circular Street. How might have this street received its name?
- Notice the Christmas tree lights on the tree in front of Skidmore Hall. Are they early for Christmas or late in taking the lights down?
- Notice the patterns and textures in the sidewalks. Take rubbings with paper and pencil. Are the cracked sidewalks beautiful or ugly? Explore the vine-covered fence. What animal evidence can you find?
- What animal foods can you find? Where was the fence made? When was it patented?
- Crush and smell the feathery leaves growing on the grass in front of the Route 9P state highway sign. This plant is yarrow and was sold in old apothecary shops as a tonic. Find other aromatic leaves along the way.
- Go east on Union Avenue. What university was once across the street?
- Where was the bus stop sign made?

- Turn north at the corner on Regent Street. What might have caused the depression in the grass along the sidewalk?
- Examine the vines on the fence carefully. Find a leaf scar where last year's leaf was attached. Find a new bud.
- Notice the frieze on the brick building ahead of you. From this clue, how might this building be used? What other clues can you find to support your theory?
- The next building, which was constructed in 1904 with the ionic columns, has a raised pattern on the side of the steps. Can you take a photo of this pattern?
- What kind of grey rock could this be?
- Which was here first, the twin oaks or the buildings on either side? How could you find out for sure?
- Return to our starting point and share some highlights of your walk with someone. Are you more aware of the potential of a city block for learning?

❑ Activity #29: Feelings From the Past

Go outside and locate natural objects and events that cause you to feel certain ways. Consider your past contacts with these parts of nature. Do past memories help shape your present-day feelings? How? Some people believe there are just four basic feelings: mad, glad, sad, and scared. Find at least one thing that causes you to experience each of these. After doing this, rank these feelings from most intense to the least intense. Was it difficult to find examples of all four feelings? Explain.

❑ Activity #30: Separating Thoughts and Feelings

Go outside and sit alone for a while. On a piece of paper, write the word "thoughts" at the top of one column and the word "feelings" in another column. Under each heading, write the thoughts and feelings you experience. Which list was longer? Which list was easier to write? Was it difficult to distinguish between thoughts and feelings?

❑ Activity #31: Feeling Words

Go outside and use your different senses of sight, hearing, touch, taste, and smell to make contacts with nature. Using a list of feelings that you can create, try to identify how you feel while doing these activities. Consider feelings, such as awed, bored, charmed, confused, delighted, excited, free, gratified, overwhelmed, proud, relaxed, reverent, skeptical, sympathetic, tense, uneasy, and wonderful. Take notes to help you share what you learn about your feelings. What thoughts came to mind as you created different feelings? Did thoughts produce feelings or did feelings produce thoughts?

❑ Activity #32: Natural Humor

Go outside and find natural objects to use as sources of inspiration for creating humor. For example, an acorn cap can be described as an oak-sprout beanie or a small bowl for hot "oakmeal." Find at least three objects and return to the group to share your natural humor. Did this humor search help you see nature in new ways? Do you look for ways to make people laugh when you are with people?

❑ Activity #33: Observing Natural Movements

Go outside and sit alone in a spot where you can observe something moving. After carefully observing the movement, return to a designated spot to meet the group. Then, share what was observed by moving in the same way. This activity can be made into a guessing game to see if the group can guess what each person observed. Did the participants become aware of something new outdoors? How did they feel, while moving like the natural object or event moved?

❑ Activity #34: Becoming Part of Your World

Imagine that you can magically become part of the world around you. Pretend that you are the wind, a tree, a blade of grass, soil, a drop of water, a rock, cloud wisp, or anything else you find outdoors. Spend a few minutes "becoming" each one and get in touch with how that feels. After you have tried several things, select the one that helped you feel the most calm and relaxed and spend more time as that object. How could you use that in other situations when you are feeling tense?

❑ Activity #35: Plant Empathy

Go outside and walk in a natural area in a way that will not harm even the smallest plant that you can see. While you are walking, be as quiet as possible and slowly place your feet so that you will not crush any plants. Using a length of string, mark a trail for others to follow that will harm the fewest number of plants growing in the area. Is it possible to walk in a natural area without destroying anything? Do we have a right to disturb living things? How can we become more empathic to non-human living things?

SOME QUESTIONS AND ANSWERS ABOUT ENVIRONMENTAL AND PEOPLE AWARENESS

- How important is it to know the names of the plants and animals before going outdoors to explore? In reality, a leader can conduct sessions in outdoor and environmental education without knowing the given names of anything outdoors. Identification by name is only one characteristic of that object. Of course, it is helpful to know some broad classes of living things, such as trees, shrubs, ferns, mosses, and lichens, but even this isn't necessary. The characteristics of the plant or animal observed through using the senses are more important than the name. Virtually hundreds of awareness activities can be led without knowing how to identify natural objects. On the other hand, knowing the specific name of a living or non-living thing will open more possibilities for program or curriculum planning.

What is the role of asking questions in leading groups outdoors? Many years ago, the late L. B. Sharp, an outdoor education pioneer, said that it is much more difficult to ask a good question to guide discovery than to give the answers to some questions already posed. The question, "How many living things can you find under this fallen log?" produces more meaningful learning than the question, "What is the name of the animal with a pair of legs on each segment?"

Open-ended questions that invite investigation allow the participants to supply more information to the decision-making process and take more responsibility for learning. Questions can also be asked for which the leader expects no answer. These rhetorical questions can focus awareness on important objects or events in nature. The question, "I wonder how many colors there are on the leaves in the fall?" can draw attention to variety in leaf coloration and tone.

- How can natural areas be used for increasing awareness and still be preserved for the future? Natural environments must be preserved if future generations are to enjoy them. They are also there to be used for people's pleasure and convenience. How can this dilemma be resolved? Any plant that is in short supply in the immediate area or on the state or national protected lists should be considered off-limits to picking or disturbing.

One general rule is that if you can see more than 100 of the same plant, it's permissible to take a few for a good use. The question then arises as to what is a good use. Perhaps, if the natural object can be made into a useful or aesthetic product, it can be picked. Also, if people can learn more about the object and, in the process, appreciate it more, it can be picked.

There are few hard and fast rules to apply to the "pick or not to pick" dilemma. The important habits of mind are gratitude, respect, and reverence for the plant. Many indigenous people believe in the idea of reciprocity – if we receive a gift, we must return a gift. Some leaders follow indigenous ways and offer a pinch of corn meal in return for picking a plant. Many young participants respond enthusiastically to this idea and quickly understand the message of reciprocity.

A survey of the flora and fauna in an area is necessary, if rare species are to be protected. The location of trails, activity fields, campsites, or future buildings should be determined with an eye to environmental impact on the plants and animals. Few animals should be kept in captivity. Perhaps, a few hardy species, such as the turtle and snake, can be kept for short periods of time for study, if the proper conditions are provided. Animals are often more appreciated in the wild rather than in a cage or terrarium. One reason to learn to identify some plants and animals is to know which are threatened with extinction because of indiscriminate picking and killing.

In summary, the following tips and suggestions can be used for leading participants in awareness activities:

- Guide people in using as many senses as possible to explore the outdoors.
- Try to see nature through the eyes of young people. Encourage role-playing, play, pretending, imagining, and creating new ways of experiencing nature.
- Respond to and encourage young people's enthusiasm and curiosity for nature. Show your own enthusiasm and curiosity whenever possible. Try not to convey your own irrational dislikes and fears of nature.
- Develop simple guidelines for collecting natural objects. Where laws and private property rights prohibit collecting, enjoy nature and leave it untouched for those who come after you. Provide opportunities for young people to gather what they find. Egg containers or plastic bags are good temporary storage places for items such as rocks, weeds, cones, and seeds. When possible, collect things that have fallen to the ground or are not living so that no living thing is harmed or destroyed. Ask permission before collecting objects from someone's property. Avoid picking up sharp objects, such as broken glass or thorns. Avoid putting anything found outside in the mouth, unless a knowledgeable person gives permission. Remember these simple words: "Let nature live in your heart, not die in your hand."
- If you don't know the name of something in nature, have the participants make up a name, based on some characteristic of that object. Don't let the lack of a name stop you from learning about it.
- Demonstrate a concern for all living things and be conscious of what young people are learning about death and decay.
- Read and provide identification books about nature and then try to find these objects outdoors. Help young people see how objects found indoors are connected to the larger world of nature outside.
- Go outside in all kinds of weather. If people are dressed properly, nature can be enjoyed throughout the whole year.
- Set aside a bulletin board or a nature table on which objects can be displayed.
- Provide numerous opportunities for people to make choices and decisions, while learning from the outdoors. Focus on the joys of exploration and discovery.
- Stress the positive aspects of nature, such as beauty, balance, harmony, variety, complexity, strength, and rebirth.

"The invariable mark of wisdom is to see the miraculous in the common."

—Ralph Waldo Emerson

GIVING CREDIT WHERE CREDIT IS DUE

The authors first encountered the idea of task cards or environmental studies cards in the 1970s, when Addison Wesley published *Essence I and Essence II* (1970/revised 1971). They were developed by the Environmental Studies for Urban Youth Project, sponsored by the American Geological Institute, and funded by the National Science Foundation. They were described as "permission slips to openness – a prime ingredient of learning."

Essence I, consisting of 78 assignment cards, dealt with the outside environment (e.g., "Find the youngest and oldest thing in the school or outside.") and the inside environment (e.g., "Keep a book of your fantasies, daydreams, nightdreams"). *Essence II*, consisting of 171 awareness cards, centered on 10 units or themes, such as "communicate," "movement," "community," "people patterns," and "enviros."

The assignments were purposely ambiguous, because the creators wanted participants to invent an understanding of the problem and then to devise a solution. The leader was cautioned to act as a support person, not a decision-maker, and let the participants follow their own paths in exploring the assignments. Both sets were accompanied by a 48-page teachers' booklet. These cards were an early version of nature and human-nature activities and were designed for urban, suburban, and rural areas.

For a more thorough treatment of indigenous approaches to reciprocity and the gathering of plants, see Robin Wall Kimmerer's book, *Braiding Sweetgrass: Indigenous Wisdom, Scientific Knowledge, and the Teachings of Plants* (2013). Her chapter, "The Honorable Harvest" goes into detail about how she decides whether or not to pick plants.

For the philosophical foundation for "Mindfulness and Coming to Your Senses: Environmental and People Awareness," be sure to see our companion book, *Humanizing Outdoor and Environmental Education*, which is described at the beginning of the Resources chapter in this book. In particular, see Chapter 3 ("Two Views of the New Nature Movement") and Chapter 4 ("Traveling the World Bearing Nature's Gift of Peace").

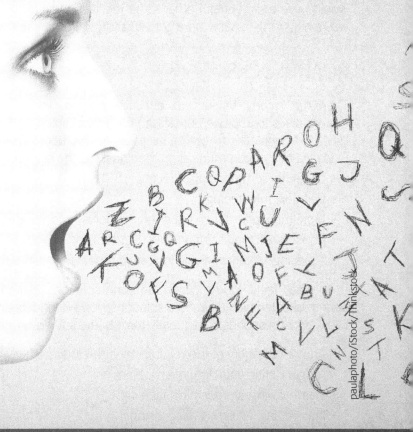

CHAPTER 3
PEOPLE MESSENGERS: DEVELOPING COMMUNICATION SKILLS

paulaphoto/iStock/Thinkstock

"I know you believe you understand what you think I said, but I am not sure you realize that what you heard is not what I meant."

—Robert McCloskey

Increasing communication skills is a difficult goal to achieve, but well worth the effort. Communicating is important in any type of human contact, and it is especially important when people live closely together over a period of time, as in a family, a classroom, a camp, or an outdoor school.

Communication is a process of translating ideas into symbols and then sending them to a receiver who interprets the idea. In this process, there are a number of things that can go wrong. How many times have you given what you thought were very clear directions to someone, only to find that she did not understand? Perhaps, the symbols you chose to represent an idea did not mean the same thing to the other person. Perhaps, you assumed that the other person knew some information you did not provide. Perhaps, the receiver of your directions had something else bothering her, and she did not listen to all or part of what you said. Or perhaps, the symbols you chose to use in giving directions—the words—were not the best. Maybe drawing a map would have been better. Perhaps, the receiver knew how to get to the destination, but was really trying to strike up a conversation to get to know you.

ROADBLOCKS

There are many barriers to effective communication and seldom do we have opportunities to improve our skills in this area. Clinical psychologist Dr. Thomas Gordon lists 12 "roadblocks to communication" in his book, *Teacher Effectiveness Training*. One category of communication roadblocks is the solution-giving responses:
- Ordering, commanding, directing
- Warning, threatening
- Moralizing, preaching, and giving "shoulds" and "oughts"
- Advising, offering solutions or suggestions
- Teaching, lecturing, giving logical arguments

It often feels good to offer someone solutions to life problems. If you have ever been presented with unwanted solutions, you will understand why the aforementioned five ways of responding frequently form barriers to communication.

Another category of the roadblocks is the judgment-giving responses:
- Judging, criticizing, disagreeing, blaming
- Name-calling, stereotyping, labeling
- Interpreting, analyzing, diagnosing

No one likes to be negatively judged, not even if it is "for her own good." One way to practice being non-judgmental is to "fire" or "suspend" the little judge that sits on the bench in your head. Try looking at people and events without judging them. You may find this difficult to do, but being temporarily non-judgmental is important if effective communication is to take place.

Another category of the roadblocks is the support-giving responses:
- Praising, agreeing, giving positive evaluations
- Reassuring, sympathizing, consoling, supporting

It might appear contradictory to present these support-giving responses as roadblocks to communication. In certain contexts, however, they may interfere with really hearing the full expression of another's feelings. Your support-giving responses may be misinterpreted as being insincere and may also take the focus away from the other person and on to yourself. There are numerous instances when support-giving is exactly what is needed, but it can sometimes interfere with effective communications.

The remaining two roadblocks are difficult to categorize:
- Questioning, probing, interrogating, cross-examining
- Withdrawing, distracting, being sarcastic, humoring, diverting

When these responses interfere with the process of conveying and interpreting the meaning of ideas among people, they are inappropriate.

NOW WHAT?

According to Virginia Satir, a noted family therapist, "Once a human being has arrived on this earth, communication is the largest single factor determining what kinds of relationships he makes with others and what happens to him in the world about him." When viewed from this perspective, you might wonder why you have not been required to take courses in communication, since you started kindergarten. It is also difficult to understand why everyone seems to have to learn so much about communication through trial and error.

Everyone experiences their environment in their own unique way. We cannot assume that any two people have an identical experience, even though they may be exposed to the same outside stimuli. When you assume that another person sees the world in exactly the same as you do, both of you can experience communication difficulties.

Each of us wears a pair of invisible-colored glasses that filter what we see in the environment. Our filters include our past experiences, as well as our feelings at the moment. Just being aware of your own feelings and needs at the moment is not enough if you need to cooperate with one or more people. You must accurately communicate these feelings and needs to others in order for them to respond to you.

You communicate with much more than words. You can also use physical touch, body movement, gestures of all kinds, facial expressions, and tone of voice. It is important to remember that people have meanings within them, not in the words they choose to use. You may want to ask yourself, "What body language and symbols would best convey the meaning inside of me to another person?"

The brief overview of the communication process in this chapter will be illustrated through the following communication activities involving nature and human nature. These activities can help to overcome communication roadblocks by focusing upon one or more of the following guidelines:

- Do not assume that any two people have identical experiences from the same stimuli. Do not assume that: (a) others know what you want from them; (b) they understand you when you tell them; or (c) you know exactly how they feel at the moment.
- We communicate with different types of body language and nonverbal signals.
- Get in touch with feelings in yourself and others in the "here and now" of present time. Look for the sometimes hidden feelings behind the words used.
- Temporarily "suspend" the judge within you in order to really hear what another person is saying. Being judgmental often interferes with good communication.
- Check out with others how they are perceiving the world around them. Be aware of the filters through which everyone views their environment.

The following activities provide opportunities to learn and practice good communication skills. These skills include: effective listening, empathizing, accurate observing, role-playing and pretending, communicating and perceiving congruence between verbal and nonverbal messages, interpreting the feelings behind the words of others, and becoming aware of your own feelings.

ACTIVITIES

❑ Activity #36: Nature Charades

Go to a particular place where a particular event is happening. It could be a tree blowing in the wind, a bird building a nest, an insect crawling on a flower, or any similar occurrence. When an event is selected, return to the group and nonverbally act it out in charade-type fashion. Different nonverbal symbols can be prearranged to help in figuring out the incident (e.g., people event, wildlife event, inanimate object event, etc.). Some familiar charade-like gestures can also be used, such as "sounds like," "number of syllables," or "correct answer." This activity can also be done while walking along a trail or a sidewalk.

❑ Activity #37: Nature Life Symbols

Form trios or quartets. Give everyone approximately 15 minutes to find objects in the environment to symbolize different aspects of their lives. It is best to select objects (e.g., fallen leaves, soil, acorns and other seeds, grass blades, rocks, sticks, litter, animal evidence, etc.) that can be transported easily back to a central meeting place and will not cause too great an impact on the ecology of the area. When the objects are gathered, arrange them into a collage on the ground to represent each person's life. The objects can also be arranged along a "life line" to depict various events and life stages. After each collage or lifeline is created, volunteers can share all or part of their stories with the others.

❑ Activity #38: Variation—Finding Yourself Outdoors

Go outside and find things that symbolize yourself. We often become aware of our surroundings, because we see parts of ourselves in objects and events. When you locate what you are asked to find, you can bring it back to share with others in one of the following ways:

- The object itself
- A sketch of the object or event
- A verbal description of the object or event

If you choose to bring back the object itself, you must follow these two rules:

- The object cannot be part of a living and growing plant.
- The object can be easily replaced where you found it, without harming it or the surroundings.

This activity has three purposes: to become more aware of your surroundings; to consider what you think is important about yourself; and to allow the members of the group to get to know you better. Please return promptly when you hear the signal and stay within the boundaries. Be sure to respect the environment as you discover more about it and yourself. Please return any objects to the places you found them after the activity. Find something that symbolizes one or more of the following:

- A skill or talent you are good at doing
- A wish for the future
- Something you would like to give to someone special
- A pleasant memory from the past
- A quality you have that helps make you a good friend

❑ Activity #39: Nature Ventriloquist

Select something that can be seen or heard from a particular spot outside. Then give that object or thing a voice and carry on a conversation between yourself and that object. For example, if you choose a cloud in the sky, the conversation might involve the following:

Cloud:"Hello down there. Don't you wish you were up here with me?"

You:"Well, you know, it might be fun."

Cloud:"Right now, I feel warm and comfortable, but it gets pretty cold at night."

You:"Yes, but what a beautiful view of the stars you have."

Cloud:"I don't feel like I have a very solid foundation in life. I wish I felt more grounded."

Try this exercise by pretending to be the cloud for a while. Take turns in conversations between yourself and the cloud. Think about how it feels to talk to a natural object. How does it feel when you are pretending to be that object? Did you learn anything about yourself? How was your object like you? Or, not like you?

❑ Activity #40: Sensory Sharing

Find a partner and decide who will be blindfolded first. The sighted person then guides the blindfolded person nonverbally to explore the environment. The object is to provide the blindfolded person with the most joyous and sensory experience possible. Care must be taken to make the exploration as safe as possible for the blindfolded person.

Among the things you could try are the following: sharing many textures, smells, and sounds; walking at different speeds and even running or skipping; sprinkling the blindfolded person with cool water from a lake or stream; shaking hands with others in the group, as they are met along the way; and just sitting unattended for a minute to experience the sounds. This nonverbal sharing of the environment can be a very satisfying experience for both partners. After 15 minutes, the partners can switch roles.

After both individuals have had an opportunity to be blindfolded, they can share their feelings on such questions as: Which role was more comfortable? What experiences created feelings, such as fear, joy, curiosity, or surprise? Did the nonverbal rule heighten or detract from the experience? If this activity were repeated, what new experience would you each provide the other? What experiences would you eliminate? What experiences helped to build trust in each other?

❑ Activity #41: Sharing Branch

Find a large, dead branch to bring inside or suspend from a support outside. Ask everyone to go outside and bring back something that they would like to share with the whole group. When each person returns, provide string and tape to attach the object to the sharing branch. After the branch is decorated with everyone's contribution, each person, in turn, explains what was hung on the branch and why it was selected.

❑ #Activity #42: Group Pictures

Give a small group of about eight persons a large sketching pad and some crayons or magic markers. Then, have them go outside and create a scene visible from where they are standing. Each person is given a chance to add one part of the scene. Then, the crayon or marker is passed to the next person. The group picture is continued, until everyone agrees that it is complete. This activity can be tried either verbally or nonverbally. This creative sharing illustrates how each person in the group sees the same scene in their own way and how each selects what is important.

❑ Activity #43: Nature Towers

Form small groups of six to eight people. Have each group go outside and find natural objects to use in building a tower. The towers can be judged for the highest, best-looking, most sturdy, and most ecologically sound. One person is selected from each group to form a panel of judges. One individual is selected from each group to observe and report on how well their group completed the task. The only materials provided to each group are a ball of string, a roll of masking tape, and some "crazy" glue. The task is to be completed in 20 minutes, with each group given an additional five minutes to plan. After the planning session, the rest of the task is to be completed without talking. After the 20 minutes of tower building is completed and judged, each group (builders, observers, and judges) can talk about their feelings and thoughts stemming from the activity.

❑ Activity #44: Environmental Trio Sharing

monkeybusinessimages/iStock/Thinkstock

Divide into small groups of three. Complete the following sequence of events to explore various aspects of communication. One person volunteers to start and be the focus person. The focus person talks for two minutes on a topic of interest. The other two people in the trio are to purposely not listen. They may ignore the focus person, ask diverting questions, or converse with each other. After two minutes, a second person in the trio becomes the focus person and the activity is repeated. After another two minutes, the third person becomes the focus person. After all three people have had an opportunity to be not-listened-to, they can share their feelings.

The first focus person then chooses another topic to talk on for two minutes. This time, the other two persons try their best to practice good listening skills. They should make eye contact with the focus person, show attentive body posture, not interrupt to share their own experiences, and concentrate on both the content and the feelings behind the words of the focus person. Subsequently, the other two individuals take their turn as the focus person. After all three people have done this, they all take time to share their feelings and thoughts.

Among the suggested topics for the focus person are the following:
- What does wilderness mean to me?
- What does it feel like to be alone in the woods?
- How can I have lots of fun outdoors?

- What is my biggest fear outdoors?
- How does it feel to climb a tree?
- What would it be like to not ever see a tree again?
- How could I use a park if I lived in the city?
- What part of the environment would I most like to save for future generations to see?

❏ Activity #45: Nature Nonsense

You can often get a lot of clues about the meaning of a word when it is used in context with other words. Each person is to go outside, and find an object and give it a nonsense name. For example, the name could be "ibbledibble" for a maple tree. Then a nonsense adjective describing that object should be invented, such as "brigetle" in place of curving. You can then write a story about that object, using both nonsense words as many times as possible. The aim of the activity is for others to guess the meaning of the nonsense noun and adjective and to figure out the object in the story. The following one such story:

> The brigetle ibbledibble stood silhouetted against the bright blue sky.
> The brigetle was gradual, but distinct. Perhaps, it was caused when the
> ibbledibble was young and bent by some playful farm boy. The brigetle
> made it easier to climb to the top of the ibbledibble. I thought only birches
> were brigetle like that, but now I know that ibbledibbles are brigetle too.

❏ Activity #46: Sound Symbols

Sounds can be translated into symbols, using words or line segments and curves. Listen to sounds in the environment and put words and line segment symbols to them. For example, a tufted titmouse might appear to call, "peter, peter, peter." Bluejays sometimes call, "jay, jay." A woodpecker tapping on a tree sounds like "ratatat tat." Translate as many sounds that you hear in the environment, using words. Line segments can be used in the following ways to represent various sounds:
- Call of a bobwhite quail
- Call of a crow
- Sound of a siren

Have people guess what makes each sound from seeing each type of symbol.

❏ Activity #47: Word and Picture Symbols

Make a list of 10 of the most noticeable parts of your surrounding environment. After making this list, compare it with the lists of others who have done the same thing, at the same time, and in the same place. How many of the things on the list were the same? How many were different?

Even if you have some of the same words listed as someone else, you cannot assume that you share the same concept that the words represent. To illustrate this point, ask everyone in the group to draw a tree. The trees that they draw will be as varied as real trees are in nature, maybe even more varied. Try writing down descriptive words about any single natural object, such as a rock, stream, stump, cloud, and bird. Because our experiences with each of these concepts differ, so will our symbols to represent them.

❑ Activity #48: Reading Feelings

Try to tune in to someone else's feelings for a while. The words another person uses may not always be a clue to their true feelings. Try to empathize with someone by walking with her from place to place, in your immediate environment. At each place, try to guess how the other person feels toward that spot. After each guess, have your partner tell you how the spot makes her feel.

As you go from spot to spot, and you learn more about how the environment affects your partner, can you empathize more accurately? Introduce natural objects to your partner and continue this empathizing exercise. Always check out how your partner is seeing and sensing the environment. Ask questions to get a better idea of how stimuli affect one another. Concentrate on how the environment affects each of you in the "here and now."

❑ Activity #49: Environmental Pictures

Mount several hundred pictures, cut from old magazines, on 5" x 8" cards. These scenes can be of rural, suburban, and urban views, environmental use and abuse, and from a wide variety of ecosystems (deserts, forests, beaches, etc.).

Each participant is directed to select about 12 cards, based on which ones create a strong feeling inside the person. This feeling could be either positive or negative. The person does not need to fully understand the reasons behind the choices at the time of selection.

After the cards are selected, they are arranged on the floor or table in front of each participant. First, the cards can be analyzed according to predominant color; type of scenery Whether the card depicts a person's past, present, or future; the feelings each picture evokes; those places a person would like to live or vacation; and good and bad environmental impact.

Later, a story can be made up about the pictures selected. The pictures can also be lined up according to the one liked most to the one liked least. The results of these ways of looking at the pictures can then be shared with others.

For further discussion with a partner or in small groups, consider the following questions:
- Which picture or pictures would you have picked from someone else's selections?
- Which pictures represent high points and challenging times in your life?
- Why did another person select a picture? Try to guess the reasons for each selection.
- Can a poem be written by combining feeling words from each of the pictures?
- What would you title each picture if you were the artist or photographer?
- How do others feel when you give them one of your pictures?

The following are examples of comments from people who had just completed this environmental picture-card activity. This will give you a taste for what can result from participating in communications skill-building activities:

- "I got in touch with some goals I am seeking and also gained confidence that I can recognize what I want. I also liked the way this activity revealed parts of my partner's life in an easy, non-threatening manner. This was a pleasant memory journey."
- "Happy for the opportunity to share part of myself with another, and vice versa. Content with pleasant memories. I would like more opportunities for sharing."
- "I felt it put me more in touch with some of the things I value—wildlife, the outdoors, skiing, and people. I would like to have been able to see more pictures."
- "I did learn something of my partner and of myself. I experienced a great deal of beauty and inspiration. I think it's a great way to teach art or science."
- "I found this be a very relaxing exercise. It allowed my mind to wander to places that I have gone to and other areas where someday I hope to be. It made me feel that my life has been full and good so far, and that there is much promise and adventure in the future. There was a lovely magical fusion between picture and imagination."

❑ Activity #50: Hearing Voices

Go outside and locate a natural object, such as a leaf, rock, or stick. When some object "speaks" to you, pick it up and have a "conversation" with it. Then, bring it back to the group to share that conversation. What did it "say"? What did you say to the object? How did you feel as you were having a conversation with that object? What benefits might result from having a conversation with nature?

❑ Activity #51: Communicating Patterns

With a partner, gather matching sets of two sticks (each a different size); four rocks (each a different size); and two leaves. The items should be matched as closely as possible. Sit back-to-back in a comfortable place, with the eight objects in front of each person. One person chooses to be the follower and the other the leader. The leader arranges the items in a pattern on the ground and then attempts to describe the arrangement to the follower. The follower tries to duplicate the same pattern, but cannot speak or look at the leader's arrangement. When the follower completes the task, she can look at the leader's pattern to see if it matches. Switch roles and repeat the activity. Discuss how this task would be different if the follower was allowed to ask questions. Repeat the activity, allowing the follower to talk and ask questions. Were there any differences in the ways the task was completed? Was communication improved during the second round? How?

❑ Activity #52: Empathy Sharing

Sit face-to-face with a partner in a comfortable place outside. Ask your partner to take several minutes to mention everything that comes into her awareness by using her senses of sight, hearing, touch, and smell. After your partner finishes, share some of your thoughts and feelings that occurred. Repeat the exercise and share your awareness with your partner. Are you better able to empathize with your partner now? Did your partner help you notice new things in your surroundings … and vice versa?

❑ Activity #53: Leaf Puzzle

Select a large leaf with a single blade (not a compound leaf with leaflets). Try to find one that is at least five inches across. Tear it into as many pieces as there are members in the small group. If the group is larger than six or eight, divide them into smaller groups. Mix up the leaf pieces and let each person select one piece of the puzzle. Without talking or signaling to each other, they must silently put the leaf back together again, starting from the top and moving to the base. The object of the game is to put the leaf back together in the shortest possible time by placing one leaf piece at a time. Designate a timer to start the group and keep time. Repeat the task by taking a new leaf piece. Try completing two leaf puzzles by combining pieces from another small group and repeating the task. What difficulties emerged? How did the group try to communicate non-verbally? Try the task again, but this time allowing verbal communication. How was this different?

❑ Activity #54: Partner Poets

With a partner go to a natural area and write a poem together. Use a standard poetic form, such as haiku, cinquain, free verse, acrostic, rhyme, senryu, tanka, or other form. Make sure that both participants in the partnership agree on the word selection as the poem is written. How was the decision made about what kind of poem to write? Was it easier to write a poem with a partner or was it more difficult than writing alone? What did you learn about your partner? How do you like your poem?

❑ Activity #55: Word Painting

Find a partner and decide which one of you will start this activity. That person is to go outside alone and find something in the environment to describe to the other. The object or natural phenomenon is to be observed carefully and described in such a way that the other person could go outside and find the real thing. The descriptive words should not reveal the identity too quickly, but be designed to create a detailed word painting of the object.

You can modify this activity by having the second person seated, facing away from the object. As the first person describes the object in detail, the second person sketches it. The sketching is to be done nonverbally, and the word painter is not allowed to see the sketch as it is being done. When the description and sketch are completed, the pair then compares it to the sketch on paper. A sharing of feelings can follow the activity. The partners could then switch roles and repeat.

Among the questions to consider in the sharing are the following:
• How did it feel to try to verbally describe an object or natural event?
• How did it feel to try to visualize that object or event?

- What kinds of descriptions were easiest? Most difficult?
- How would this activity be different if the sketcher could give feedback to the word painter?

How would this be different if the word painter could see what the sketcher was doing and make corrections along the way?

SUMMARY

This chapter outlined several of the reasons for the importance of including communication skills in your group, camp, or school program. A number of communication concepts were discussed, along with some barriers to effective communication. The activities provide opportunities for participants to learn about communication by practicing verbal and nonverbal skills.

The outdoor environment provides a unique medium for learning about communication. Often, a new setting can facilitate skill-building and enable the transfer of these skills to other areas of life. Because some of these activities may be new to participants and involve a level of risk, some people may be reluctant to try them. As a leader, you must demonstrate that the goals of the activities are important and that the means for reaching these goals can be fun, as well as beneficial.

We encourage you to modify some of the activities, if, for any reason, they do not feel quite right for your leadership style or for the participants. We believe that effective leaders must be convinced of the value of introducing structured activities, before they can be successful in reaching communication objectives.

> *"What you do speaks so loudly that
> I cannot hear what you say."*
>
> —Ralph Waldo Emerson

GIVING CREDIT WHERE CREDIT IS DUE

We have drawn on a few of the ideas of Thomas Gordon and Virginia Satir in introducing these nature and human nature communication activities. For more depth in preparing to lead these and other experiences, leaders will benefit from further reading. See the Resources chapter in our companion book, *Humanizing Outdoor and Environmental Education*, which is described at the beginning of Chapter 8 in this book.

CHAPTER 4
PEOPLE HARMONY: BUILDING A SENSE OF COMMUNITY

"I like a forest's way of living with a river."

—Dana Robinson

Pixland/Pixland/Thinkstock

A community is much more than a collection of individuals in one place. People become a community when they cooperate in living, playing, and working together. They agree on certain human values and goals, however few or general in nature. Building a collection of people into interdependent and cooperative community members does not just happen. Community-building is both an art and a skill, and, as such, must be planned in order to achieve the expected ends. This is true, whether it is a classroom in a school, an outdoor program, a camp, an organization's staff, or any other group that meets in an ongoing way.

Leaders generally agree that one important aim of outdoor education and humanistic education is to help people reach more of their potential as human beings. Camps and outdoor schools have been established to facilitate change in the direction of more effective and happier group members. Often, it is assumed that personal and social growth occur automatically in outdoor settings and few plans are made to achieve a sense of unity and cohesiveness. Much of the focus in outdoor programming is on knowledge and skill areas, such as ecology, crafts, astronomy, map reading, swimming, or hiking. However, if the goal is better human relations, more thought must be given to community-building techniques. This should be reflected in the scheduled activities and planned time periods of the environmental program.

Whenever individuals come together for the first time in a new setting, they experience numerous questions about themselves in relation to the group. Among those questions are the following:

- How do others see me?
- Who will become my close friends?
- Who can I really trust here?
- Will others accept me?
- How long will it take to feel a part of the group?
- What are the others in the group really like?
- Who has the most power in this group?
- What will happen while we are here?
- How will we work together?
- What will I be like when I leave?

These questions are shared by many individuals and can be answered as a community evolves. A fully functioning community is characterized by several elements, including:

- Community members understand their purpose for being together—their goals are clear.
- They know the rules under which they will be operating and, in turn, know their areas of freedom.
- They understand that they have a degree of power in decision-making and a feeling that their opinions count.

- They know that although leadership responsibilities will be shared, the staff has the "ultimate responsibility" for the health and safety of the group. The staff must be respected and trusted.
- Trust must extend throughout the entire community for growth to occur. A degree of safety and comfort must exist for a community to function effectively.
- Mutual caring is the key to success in moving from a collection of individuals to a growing, effective community.

Community-building activities must be carefully thought out in order to achieve the desired results. One way of developing a sense of community is to increase the feeling of cooperation among all group members—competition must be downplayed in the program. The spirit of a cooperative activity is reflected in the question: How can we all gain by having fun together, while we learn more about ourselves and others?

In a cooperative program, activities are structured so that everyone wins. Even in the case of an activity that results in one winner, everyone could experience a degree of success in the process leading to the one winner. No prizes or awards are given to a select few. Rewards of personal satisfaction and fun are the prizes for all. Individual differences are recognized and applauded. Everyone is not expected to contribute to an activity in the same way. Each contribution can be viewed as building to the success of the whole activity.

In reality, some individuals are opposed to this program philosophy. Sometimes, these critics voice objection to an emphasis on cooperation, because they feel that young people need to be trained for the competitive, dog-eat-dog world around them. We contend that our society reflects cooperation to a far greater degree than it does competition. Consider how families, churches, industries, schools, community service organizations, and other elements of society function together to meet their goals.

Other critics of cooperative programming contend that young people want competition in games and activities. We believe that most human beings tend to request the familiar pastimes and games, rather than the unknown. Competitive activities are what they know best, because their culture has encouraged and supported them most. If people experience more cooperative activities, we believe that then they will request them over the competitive ones. Arguably, the few people who are the winners in competitive games are the only ones requesting their perpetuation.

In this chapter, we explore some community-building activities in which cooperation is the glue. As you read and try them out with groups, strive to discover some other common elements of community-building activities. There are many activities that encourage creative expression, while also fostering a sense of community in people. These activities pool the creative talents of the group so that each can contribute in a special way.

ACTIVITIES

❑ Activity #56: Human Treasure Hunt

This activity provides a great opportunity to discover the human treasures in your group. Give participants a "Find people who …" sheet that invites them to find out more about others in the group. Encourage folks to follow two guidelines: write down the names of people who fit each description; and there is a limit of two notations per customer. In other words, after you have written one person's name twice, then say, "see you later," and keep on trucking to other group members. As such, the underlying goal is to "share the wealth" of the human treasures. The following is a taste of some playful and serious statements that could appear on the human treasure hunt—of course, we encourage you to make up your own that would be appropriate to your group (and/or have the participants create the statements):

- Find two people who could have used another hour's sleep last night.
- Find three people who wonder "what they want to be when they grow up."
- Find two people who like to fish.
- Find four people who have a different astrological sign than you.
- Find two people who have taken time "to smell the flowers" (literally).
- Find one person who had the same favorite Halloween costume as a kid as you.
- Find three people who have painted an outdoor scene.
- Find two people who face a similar kind of stress as you. Lend a listening ear.
- Find four people who have a good balance between "work" and "play" in their lives. Find out how they do it.
- Find three people who can hum the *Jeopardy* theme song. Lend a childlike ear as they do it.
- Find four people who love to take photographs in the great outdoors.
- Find two people who have been an upstander, rather than a bystander, when someone else was being bullied? Ask them how they handled the situation.
- Find two people who have the same size thumb as you. Thumb wrestle someone— the best two-out-of-three.
- Find four people who go shopping at the grocery store with a cloth bag to avoid the "paper or plastic?" question.
- Find three people who have the same color eyes as you.
- Find five people who have done something positive for the environment. Find out what it was and feel free to add it to your repertoire.
- Find four people who have the same favorite comedian or cartoon as you. Share a laugh or two.

This activity can then springboard into fun discussions and connections in pairs and/or in the whole group, as a way to build on what you have in common and to respect the differences—both of which are essential to building community.

❑ Activity #57: Native American Totem

Group cooperation can occur at various points, while erecting a totem pole to depict the life of the community. First, select a tree that not only meets the requirements of a totem but can be cut down without significantly affecting the ecology of the area. Then, select a site for the totem and drag the tree there. With chisels or pocket knives, take turns carving the bark to make the totem symbols. Cutting away more than the bark and actually sculpting the wood is much more time-consuming and requires more skill, but makes for a longer lasting piece of art. After each community member has had a chance to carve a symbol into the totem, a hole must be dug, and the pole lifted into place. After the totem is erected, plan a campfire in which everyone takes a part.

❑ Activity #58: Flag or Banner Design

You can design and make a flag or banner that depicts important goals for your program or curriculum. The process starts with a group meeting to brainstorm ideas for color, layout, and symbols. For the flag or banner to truly represent the community, a consensus should be reached on the final design. Reaching consensus takes time, but the point is to decide on a flag or banner that everyone can accept with pride.

The designs and colors can be applied to a piece of material in various ways. Native dyes can be applied directly or can be used to tint wool, which can be embroidered. Simple block prints can be made by carving potato halves with designs. The community members can make the many decisions necessary to complete the flag or banner.

If this project seems too large for the time allotted, substitute a large, flat piece of driftwood or a split log for the fabric. The participants select their own symbols and initials to burn into the wooden plaque. If a wood burner is unavailable, a large nail fitted with a wooden handle can be heated in the fire until cherry red and used to burn designs. You can hang the finished product on the wall or over the fireplace mantle as a reminder of another group effort resulting in a successful project.

❑ Activity #59: Group Weaving

Group weaving can be fun and produce surprisingly aesthetic results. Different types of looms may be used. Everyone participating should see the loom to judge the proper size of the materials, and then go outside to gather them. The materials can be added in whatever sequence the group decides will make an appealing pattern and texture. We have used a simple grass mat loom and 24-inch sticks driven upright into the ground.

Nine sticks are needed. Two rows of four sticks each, about three inches apart, are driven about four to six inches into the ground. The two rows are as far apart as the grass mat will be long. Warp cords are attached, connecting the four sticks to the one across from them. An additional set of four warp cords are attached to the rear four sticks, and the other ends attached to a crossbar (the ninth stick). This arrangement forms a movable set of cords to hold bunches of dry grass, sticks, roots, or other material. With an up-and-down and back-and-forth motion of the crossbar, the material is woven into a mat or wall hanging, representing the group's creative effort.

In another type of simple loom, warp cords are attached to low-hanging branches. Grasses and other "found" materials can be woven between alternate warp cords to form an outdoor-nature weaving. The key to community-building, weaving projects is to make them a cooperative event, using native materials.

❑ Activity #60: Group Sketching

Community members can work together on a sketch, each person adding something unique. This activity can be done with a group of as many as 20, if the paper is large enough. Smaller groups of about six or eight can work on a piece of paper at the same time, if it is large enough. We use 35-inch by 44-inch newsprint, because it is relatively inexpensive and large enough. Crayons are especially useful, but any medium may be utilized for the group sketch. Each person, in turn, can add a sketch that builds on the idea of the previous people.

We have found that it is fun to make a sketch map of our campsite and fill in drawings of the community members engaged in their favorite activities. Directions can be given to do the sketch nonverbally. This type of activity can produce some very interesting results from those people who depend heavily on speech to communicate. After the sketch is completed, the group members can profit by sharing their thoughts and feelings from before, during, and after the exercise. The sketches can be hung on the wall for all to enjoy and learn about others.

❑ Activity #61: Community Newsletter

We have found that a newsletter is a positive force in building a sense of community. This project can involve all of the group members, who each contribute in their own way. Writers can do straight reporting of events, interviews, crossword puzzles, creative writing of poems and stories, advice columns, editorials, or selections from personal journals. Artists can provide sketches, diagrams, maps, and other visuals. Layout and production people can plan the layout, organize the sequence, as well as type, reproduce, and collate the final product. Special sections might be included, such as names and addresses of everyone, birthdays, graffiti (the kind that focuses on the positive aspects of the community), and appreciations of individuals. From start to finish, the newsletter helps build the community and provides a special memory after the experience is over.

❑ Activity #62: Movement and Creative Expression

Wherever possible, outdoor areas can be used for movement activities. The space and fresh air are only two reasons why. It is very important to experience the real objects and processes that inspire creative movement. Movement becomes easier and more connected to the environment among the grasses, trees, wind, clouds, streams, and animals.

The body can express beauty through movement and provide a constructive outlet for physical energy. Gather a group together and interpret the surroundings through body movement. Move like different kinds of trees in the wind, like some of the local animals, like seeds falling from plants, or like water flowing in a stream. Pretend that you are walking through a swamp as the water and mud become gradually deeper. Also walk on ice, between puddles, and through briars. Pretend you are climbing a cactus plant. Imitate a hiker climbing a mountain, rappelling down a steep cliff, or walking at night, without a flashlight in the woods.

You can practice free expression to music. We have used a kalimba to provide background music for creative movement. The possibilities for movement exercises related to the outdoors are almost unlimited.

❏ Activity #63: Cooperative Nature Trail

A nature trail is a path that leads people to greater understanding and awareness of the outdoors. Various stops along the way (stations) are usually labeled with words or numbers to guide people. Instead of having the nature expert design and label the nature trail, we have found that everyone has some insight or observation to share.

Approach this project from the viewpoint of helping others to look at the environment through your eyes. You do have a unique way of looking at the world, because of your use of the senses and your past experiences. You can reveal nature to others by stating facts and concepts about objects or events, or by asking questions about the environment around the station. Both techniques are effective, and we have used them successfully.

Giving facts and concepts requires that the senses of observation, touch, smell, hearing, and sometimes taste be brought into play. Information can also be obtained from books or by asking people who know. The goal of all information about nature should be to relate these facts and concepts to the life of the trail walker.

Try your hand at asking questions that will lead people to new discoveries along the trail. We call this a "Question Trail." Questions, such as, "What lives under this log?" or "What does the smell of this plant remind you of?" often open new doors. It is sometimes more difficult to ask good discovery questions than to give facts and concepts about natural objects and events. If each community member prepared information or questions about only one station, there would be much to share with everyone.

This group project starts with the selection of the site and trail route and ends with sharing what people create at each station. Again, there are different ways for everyone to contribute to the project. Group members could write poems, draw sketches, ask questions, or give facts and concepts at each assigned or chosen station.

❏ Activity #64: All-Night Vigil

The all-night vigil is a community project that provides for new experiences, while contributing to the total group. Start by explaining a new way to cook, using hot coals buried underground. To do this, first dig a hole about three-feet deep and large enough to hold cast iron Dutch ovens with food for the entire community.

Then, ask everyone who wishes to participate in watching a fire for one-hour shifts to sign up for a time slot during the night. People can pair or trio together during each shift. The fire is watched all night and fuel is added as needed. In the morning, the food is placed in the Dutch ovens and covered over with hot coals and soil about two-feet deep. By evening, the food is done, and then it is uncovered and eaten for dinner.

Everyone who watches the fire can feel a special sense of having helped to prepare the meal. The anticipation, combined with big appetites, helps make the occasion a memorable event. For some, the fire vigil provides the first opportunity to be outdoors during the early morning hours. The camaraderie and the natural environment are special features of this activity.

❏ Activity #65: Stream Walk

If you are fortunate enough to have a stream in the area, take a group stream walk. All you need are some old clothes and footwear that you do not mind getting wet. The whole group enters a stream and walks right down the middle. Depending on the type of stream, adventures abound and many opportunities arise for helping each other. One rule is that the group must stay together, periodically waiting for the slowest movers to catch up.

The purpose of the walk is not to get it over with quickly, but to enjoy the journey and learn something about the group members. If the stream becomes deep enough to be over the heads of the shorter people, water-safety procedures must be taken. It is always a good idea for staff with lifesaving skills to be in the lead, as well as to have some trained personnel follow behind the group. We have found this activity to be one of the best group-building adventures we have ever done. If a stream is not available, the same sense of cooperation and adventure can be achieved by taking a bee-line walk through a park or wilderness area.

❏ Activity #66: Compass Bee-Line Hike

A topographic map of the area and magnetic compasses are necessary for this activity. Sight a destination on the map and take a compass bearing. It is best to choose a target that is not more than a mile or two away, because there is always a certain amount of error along the travel route. It is also best to choose a relatively large target, like a mountain or lake. Buildings and old foundations are good destinations, but they take a greater degree of accuracy to locate. As in the stream hike, the group must stay together, as they move overland through the woods.

❏ Activity #67: Gift Giving

Selecting and giving a gift that suits a person is a skill, as well as an enjoyable activity. You might set aside a block of time for the exchange of gifts that are handmade. Alert community members a few days in advance and have everyone draw the name of someone else. In the following days, everyone prepares their gifts secretly, so that the intended recipients do not see the gifts.

Most of the items can be made partly or entirely from natural materials found around the area. Items, such as weavings, macramé necklaces and bracelets, wood carvings, homemade blueberry jelly, bread, polished driftwood, nature mobiles, pottery, original poetry and artwork, terraria, and games with native materials can be made with pride and given with pleasure. The gifts can be exchanged, one at a time, in the center of the group. Each person as they are giving and receiving can be the focus for a minute or two.

❏ Activity #68: Creativity Night

One evening can be devoted to sharing the creativity within each person. Everyone has something that they can do that requires creative talent. Each person, in turn, can present whatever they wish to share. Sometimes, groups of people put on skits or pantomimes. Songs, poems, skill demonstrations, musical compositions, or any other personal contribution can result in a pleasant evening for all.

Performing in front of a group is usually a scary thing for most people. We suggest talking about these feelings before the performance, and discussing the idea of taking risks in a supportive atmosphere. We encourage you to try, despite the fear of making mistakes. Of course, no one should be forced, if they do not wish to participate. After every performance, encourage active appreciation of each person.

❏ Activity #69: Sensory Feast

Eating together can be a special event. A sensory feast, when carefully planned, can make eating a community-building event also. A sensory feast consists of foods that are carefully chosen for color, taste, texture, sound when chewed, and significance. Foods, such as nuts, raisins, cheese, apples, brown sugar, limes, melon, pudding, fruit juices, tomatoes, and green peppers, as well as many others can provide sensory delights. You can highlight the sense of taste by closing your eyes as a partner feeds you contrasting tastes—bitter and sweet or salty and sour. If the pace of the meal is slow, readings and songs can be interspersed, and if the table and room are appropriately decorated, the meal can become a ceremonial dinner.

❏ Activity #70: Earth Day

On a selected day, stress ecology and the environment. Gather the group together and exercise the senses by guiding awareness. Touch your skin with different plant textures, smell the soil, listen for a minute to the sounds of nature, and taste edible plants. Smaller groups can pantomime an environmental story or do a dance. Music can be played and sung. Readings can stress a closeness and dependence upon nature and lifestyles, which cause a minimal impact on the land and other resources. Once the theme is chosen, creative minds will take over to produce a many-faceted performance.

❑ Activity #71: Group Living Tasks

Although group living chores, such as cooking, doing dishes, cleaning latrines, cleaning tents and cabins, getting water, and other basic essentials are not usually considered part of a scheduled camping program, they can contribute greatly to a sense of community. These tasks are essential for comfort and health and are therefore important. If the chores are shared and rotated, everyone will get a feeling of contributing to the functioning of the whole community. We suggest that staff and participants alike share in the work and that a fair system of assigning or choosing the tasks be decided upon by the entire community.

❑ Activity #72: Rituals and Ceremonies

Rituals and ceremonies that become a part of the daily or weekly activities are very important in building an identification with the community. Many camps or schools inherit traditions that bind everyone together. Each program must encourage traditional rituals and ceremonies that are still valued, as well as develop new ones when appropriate.

Two rituals that have been important to us have been friendship circles and validation circles. In the friendship circle, everyone joins hands, while someone reads an appropriate quote or speaks on an issue that is current. A validation circle consists of focusing upon each individual in turn and telling how she is appreciated and what special strengths the community members see in that person. You might consider how to build these kinds of rituals and ceremonies around daily events (e.g., waking up, eating meals, going to bed, etc.) and special occasions (e.g., birthdays, trips, last day of the program, orientation, etc.).

Purestock/Thinkstock

❑ Activity #73: Befriending a Place and Person

One way to make friends is to ask questions to find out as much as possible about someone. You can make friends with a place in the same way. With a partner you don't know very well, select a place outdoors and attempt to find out as much as you can about it. After you have answered the following questions about the place, ask these same questions of each other:
- What is one thing that makes this place/person special?
- What is one characteristic of the place/person that is unforgettable?
- What is one thing about the place/person that helps you feel comfortable?
- What is one thing about this place/person that you trust?
- What is one of the most likeable things about the place/person?

    Can you think of other questions to ask about the place/person? If so, ask them. Did you get to know the place and person better? Explain.

❑ Activity #74: Ecology Concepts

Divide into groups of six to eight participants. The leader meets with each small group separately and whispers an ecology concept to them. Then, each group finds evidence of their concept in nature. After a planning session, each group silently acts out the concept and the others try to guess what it is. Some possible concepts include the following:
- Plants decaying
- Water cycle
- Food chains
- Plant succession
- Plants slowing erosion
- Evidence of animals eating plants

❑ Activity #75: Needing Others

Go outside and find evidence of some living thing needing something else. Then, return and share what you found with the group. Can you find anything in nature that doesn't need something else? Do you need others in the community to help you meet some of your needs? Explain.

GROUP PROBLEMS

Most of the following group problems are challenges for developing self and group empathy, teamwork, and other human relations-related aspirations. Stories and role-playing situations may be used to motivate the group, and the activities can be adjusted according to the group size, age, time available, and the situation. Many of the activities can be utilized whether inside or outside. An important ingredient of these group problems is the discussion process or reflection/review that follows the attempted solution(s). This gives the participants a chance to interpret and internalize their experience.

❏ Activity #76: The Clock

Begin by having your group stand in a circle and hold hands. The object is for the group to rotate clockwise 360 degrees in one direction and then go 360 degrees back to the start. The goal is to see how quickly the group can complete the problem. Time each attempt and stop the activity, if anyone breaks her grip with another. Group cooperation is obviously essential. Sweatshirts or other markers are placed at both "6 o'clock" and "12 o'clock" inside the circle, so the group has reference points for starting and finishing.

❏ Activity #77: Line-Ups

- Number line—Members of the group are blindfolded and quietly given a number. The participants line themselves up numerically, without talking. Time may be allotted for planning before the numbers are assigned, if desired.
- Birthday line—Members of the group must arrange themselves according to the month and day of birth, without talking.
- Animal line—Members of the group are blindfolded and quietly given the name of an animal. The group members must then arrange themselves in a line according to animal size from small to large, using only the noises of the animals. No normal verbal communication is permitted.

❏ Activity #78: Artist-Clay Model

Break into groups of three. Person #1 is blindfolded and is the artist. Person #2 assumes some distinct position and is the model. Person #3 is the clay. The artist must move the clay into the same position as the model.

❏ Activity #79: Snail

The group forms a long line with their hands joined. The line begins to coil at one end, until the entire line is in a tight spiral similar to the shape of a snail. The group may move as a unit, and then uncoil and coil the opposite way.

❏ Activity #80: People Tree

If an appropriate climbing tree can be found, the group is required to get everyone in it. More challenging variations can be presented by having one person labeled "injured" and unable to move, or by having a cup of water (representing TNT) passed from the bottom person to the top person, without it being spilled.

❏ Activity #81: Blind Square

Place pegs, mallet, and rope on the ground and have one-half of the participants put on blindfolds. In this activity, the non-blindfolded participants should try to direct the blindfolded participants, so that they are able to construct a square with the rope, using the four pegs as corner posts. Members without blindfolds may not touch the equipment.

❑ Activity #82: Alarm Clock

Two people connected by locked elbows pretend that they are an alarm clock that is set to wake everyone in the middle of the night. They will "ring," if they move the position of their feet, if they are separated, or if anyone talks. The remaining group members must carry "the alarm clock" 20 feet in order to turn it off. Discuss how this problem was solved.

❑ Activity #83: Trust Circle

One blindfolded person is placed in the center of a circle. Holding her feet stationary, she relaxes, falls backwards, and is moved around the circle by group members. Group members take turns in the center. The purpose is to develop group cohesiveness and individual trust in the group.

❑ Activity #84: Trust Fall

You can do an effective trust exercise by asking someone to stand on something, such as a stump, platform, or a ladder rung, approximately four or five feet off the ground and fall backward into the arms of the group. There should be at least 10 to 12 individuals standing on level ground to act as catchers. To increase the commitment of the person who is falling, ask her to close her eyes before and during the fall. The faller should keep her arms close to the side of the body and fall with the body held rigidly, i.e., not bending at the waist. If the falling person bends at the waist, all the force of the fall is concentrated in one small area and makes catching more difficult. The two lines of catchers stand shoulder-to-shoulder, facing one another. Hands are extended, with the palms up, so they are alternated and juxtaposed to form a safe landing area. Catchers should not hold hands with each other.

❑ Activity #85: The Four Pointer

The object is to attempt to get a group of seven people across a 30-foot area, using only four points of contact with the ground. There are three rules: all seven people must start at the marked starting line and end at the finish line; no props (boards, logs, wagons) may be used; and all seven people must be in contact with each other, as they progress across the ground.

A large group can be divided into many groups of seven. Have all of the groups make the attempt, simultaneously, so they will discover solutions independently. This problem can also be done other ways, such as with five people on three points. A variation of this problem can also be created by constructing "a monster," with only a certain number of legs and arms touching the ground (the number depends on the number of participants in a group), and move it a certain distance.

❑ Activity #86: Ten-Member Pyramid

This activity challenges you to build a symmetrical pyramid with a group of 10 people, as quickly and efficiently as possible. There are two rules: timing begins when the problem has been given and ends when the final person tops off the apex; and only a 4-3-2-1 person pyramid is considered symmetrical.

❑ Activity #87: All Aboard

The object is to get all members of the group on a platform (stump, board, tee-shirt, etc.) at one time. There are two rules: in order to be on the platform, a person must have both feet off the ground; and the group must hold in position for five seconds. You can motivate the group by challenging them to quickly escape a hypothetical wave of hot peanut butter, leaking from a broken storage tank on the hill.

❑ Activity #88: Reach for the Sky

Challenge your group to make a mark as high as possible on a wall or smooth tree trunk with a piece of chalk or tape. The group is not allowed to use the tree or wall as an aid to climbing, but simply as a support. The group members must be connected by touching in some way throughout the activity. Proper spotting techniques are extremely important. As a variation, you can have participants mark their territory in the same manner as a male bear would scratch a tree trunk.

❑ Activity #89: People Pass

You can use this activity during the early part of community-building. The group forms two lines, facing each other. One person stands in front of the line and goes first by lying backward and being picked up by the rest of the people in front of the line. The first person is then passed gently along the line to the end. When the person is lowered to the ground, she takes a position at that point, ready to receive the next person, who is being passed down toward the end of the line. Everyone who wishes to participate is passed down the line, until each participant has had a turn. Reluctant people should not be forced to take a turn, but they should be told convincingly that they will be cared for safely, if they try.

❑ Activity #90: Human Knot

The group stands in a tight circle. People then grasp one hand from a person across from them. When this task is done, ask them to grasp another hand, without letting go of the first one. The only rule is that no one should grasp both hands of the same individual or the hands of the person on their immediate right or left. A human knot has been formed by everyone clasping hands.

The object of this puzzle is to unwind, without unclasping hands, until either a circle is formed again or a figure eight is formed. On rare occasions, we have seen two interlocking circles formed when everyone unwinds. This activity usually evokes much laughter and provides a great sense of accomplishment, when the group succeeds. This exercise becomes more difficult, as the group size increases beyond 15 people.

❑ Activity #91: The Diminishing Load

The goal is to move a group or series of teams across an open field as quickly as possible. The distance can vary with the estimated strength of the groups. The activity has five rules: to cross the open area, a person must be carried; the carrier must return and be carried himself; the only person allowed to walk across the open area is the last person; if the carried person touches the ground while being transported, both members must return to the start; and the number of people being carried and carrying can vary with the strength and/or imagination of the group, i.e., one-to-one is not the only way. You can change the objective by having the entire group move across the distance in as few trips as possible (this changes the emphasis from speed to efficiency).

❑ Activity #92: Happy Landings

Explain that this is a group activity, designed to test concentration and the ability to give and take directions. You will need two volunteers—one a rower and the other a dockworker. The rower will be trying to maneuver a "boat" through a rock-strewn channel and land at the dock by walking backwards and blindfolded. Explain that the rower is the lone survivor from a ship that sank. She was blinded in the explosion, but escaped in a small rowboat.

The dockworker who saw the explosion is now trying to guide the blind rower to safety. The other participants are to be the rocks and channel sides. Some of them should stand in two lines along the channel (boundaries), while the others (rocks) may stand, kneel, or sit at random in the channel area.

When the rower docks successfully, or bumps into a rock or the channel boundary, both she and the dockworker lose their turn and must choose replacements. While the new rower is being blindfolded, the "rocks" should change positions in the channel.

The game continues until everyone has a turn at being rower or dockworker. When everyone has had a chance to participate as a rower or dockworker, have the group sit in a circle and talk about the experience. Some questions that might be useful for starting the discussion include the following:
- Did the dockworkers find it easier to give directions after they had seen several people try?
- How did it feel to be the rower blindfolded and walking backwards?
- Which commands were easiest to understand?
- Which were hardest?
- Did the rowers trust the dockworkers?
- Did the "rocks" want the rowers to make it?
- Which rowers went farthest?
- What accounts for this?

❏ Activity #93: Haudenosaunee Stick Passing

Background note: Haudenosaunee is the name that the native people use for their Iroquois confederacy. It means, "people who build a house." This group of Native Americans is made up of the Mohawk, Seneca, Onondaga, Oneida, Tuscarora, and Cayuga nations. This game was first taught to one of the authors as a Seneca game, but probably all members of the confederacy played it.

The participants are divided into two equal groups and are directed to sit on the ground in two lines, closely bunched together. A smooth stick, about two- or three-feet long, is given to each leader in the line. They are all either blindfolded or told to close their eyes and not to speak while passing the stick. At a starting signal, the stick is passed overhead with two hands to the back of the line. When it reaches the last person, she passes the stick toward the front on her right side. When it reaches the front, it is passed toward the back along the left side of the line. When it reaches the back person again, it is passed forward with two hands overhead toward the front. When it reaches the front person in the line, the lead person says, "Dahnayto," the Mohawk word meaning, "now I am finished." This activity can be practiced first, while the participants are sighted, so they know the passing pattern.

To be successful, the participants in each line must depend upon non-verbal clues to complete the task. Some in the group will see the game as competitive, trying to be the first group to finish. Others in the group will see the game as cooperative, trying to work together smoothly and quickly. These two ways of viewing the game will provoke some interesting reflecting/reviewing discussions. How will the participants view this task? Does this way of viewing tasks carry over into other activities in their lives? What are the pros and cons of each way of seeing the task?

❏ Activity #94: Occupying Space

Find an open space in a field or on pavement and try to take up as much space with your body as you can. You must stay in the same spot as you do this. Then, try to take up as little space as possible. Observe how others solve these problems. Then, choose a partner and try to take up the most and least space together. After doing this, stay with your partner and join two others and repeat the task. Then, the four of you join with four more, then eight more, etc., each time doing the same thing. Did you become aware of your need for personal space by doing this activity? How important is personal space to you?

❏ Activity #95: Nature's Engineers

Divide the group into teams of three to four people. Select a nonliving material that is abundant in the area, such as leaves, stones, sticks, or other material. Using the same materials, assign each group to build the tallest structure possible within a set time limit. The participants must adhere to the following rules:
• Each person must take a turn in placing only one item at a time.
• Everyone must agree to add an item, or it cannot be added.

- If building stops, the group must reach a consensus before continuing.
- If the structure falls, it must be started again from the beginning.

After 10 or 15 minutes, the group with the tallest structure gets the tongue-in-cheek "nature's engineers award"—one of the items used in the construction. Did all the groups follow the rules? Did any of the groups try to reach a consensus, if the building stopped? What problems arose in doing this task? Were some people more concerned about what other groups were doing than building their structure?

❑ Activity #96: Alien Creatures

Pretend that your small group of four has formed into an alien creature. Join each group of four participants by linking elbows. Each group will explore their surroundings by using the senses of hearing, touching, seeing, and smelling. Have each member draw a "sense" card to assign her to a sense. This pick is the only sense they can use while exploring. Move as one alien creature to different locations, so everybody can contribute their powerful sense to explore the area. After completing the task, discuss the results. What difficulties arose? How did the individuals work together? Did the individuals focus only on their assigned sense? How did exploring in this way help others in the group?

❑ Activity #97: Mobile Happening

Go outside and find objects in nature that can be suspended on a string or a thread to make mobiles. You may wish to bring back items, such as evergreen cones, lichen, fungi, bark, husks, acorns, pods, and dry grasses, as well as many other pieces of nature. (Be aware and beware of destroying and uglifying living things in the environment.) Be sure to collect some dead twigs and branches for the cross-pieces of the mobile. After everyone has collected an assortment of objects, start the mobile happening by hanging a piece of strong thread, fishing string, or monofilament from either the ceiling or an overhead branch outside.

In turn, participants add their contribution to the ever-growing mobile. As each crosspiece or object is tied on, the rest of the group shows appreciation in any way they wish. To make the mobile happening more interesting, you and the other individuals could choose an object that represents a quality you admire about yourself. You could also select objects on the basis of beauty, past associations, favorite color, or any other criteria. When the mobile is completed, it will hang as a reminder of the lives of the people in the community. If there are more than 20 people in the group, more than one mobile happening can take place at the same time.

FOLLOW-THROUGH ON ACTIVITIES

Thinking about and discussing each part of a group problem is essential, if the aims of the community-building activities are to be met. The exercises can easily become just fun and physical experiences, without the additional educational benefit. Evaluation and discussion can take many forms. Questions, such as the ones presented in Activity #92 (Happy Landings) might be considered. Other examples of possible questions include the following:

❑ Problem-solving:
- What problems did we encounter in solving the task?
- Did we use the best method for solving the problem?
- How could the problem have been solved more rapidly?

❑ Group functions:
- Did everyone in the group participate? Why or why not?
- Who provided leadership in the group? Did everyone who wanted to lead have an opportunity to do so?
- How many people in the group provided suggestions to solve the problem? Were everyone's suggestions heard?
- Did the group help each other? How could people be more helpful?
- What different kinds of contributions were made in the group to solve the problems (physical, emotional, mental, etc.)?

❑ Individual functions:
- Did you enjoy the experience? Why or why not?
- Did you feel the group accepted your ideas and involved you in the task?
- What contributions did you make to the group?
- How would you like to change your contributions next time?

❑ Wrap up and transfer of learning:
- What did you learn from the group problem? About solving problems? About yourself? About working with others?
- Share your completion of the following sentences:
  - ✓ I relearned …
  - ✓ The people in this group …
  - ✓ I was especially proud of …
  - ✓ After solving each group problem, I felt …

Since a community is a group of organisms gathered together in close association under common rules and beliefs, achieving a sense of community is a process that is dynamic and ongoing. Groups of people never fully achieve the goal of an ideal community. However, they can approach it.

People generally behave on the basis of what they believe. If people agree that a sense of community is a desirable goal, they are often willing to work toward that end. The development of a sense of community depends upon the extent to which people believe in some of the following ideas:

- That they are relatively safe from emotional and physical harm. They feel relatively secure and trusting of others
- That *they* are worthwhile, likeable, and competent people, who deserve the best out of life
- That *other people* are worthwhile, likeable, and competent people who deserve the best out of life
- That they have a great amount of control over their lives, within the structure of the community rules
- That they are clear on much of what is important to them and have a realistic plan to achieve what is important
- That the skill of empathizing with others is important (the ability to step inside others' shoes and view the world in a similar way)
- That the skill of separating their own thoughts and feelings is important
- That honest and direct communication helps most relationships more than dishonest and indirect communication
- That conflict with others can improve human relationships, if dealt with in the proper ways
- That supporting people and telling them what is appreciated about them is more important than criticizing them
- That human diversity in values can stimulate growth, rather than stifle it
- That there should be a "give and take" in human interaction and that sometimes you win, sometimes you lose, and many times, everybody can win
- That cooperation is essential in community-building

If you would like to evaluate your curriculum or program to determine the extent to which it reflects some elements of a sense of community, use the following checklist:

❑ Does my curriculum or program:
- Emphasize cooperation more than competition?
- Provide time for people to develop new and common interests, as well as communicate their present common interests?
- Provide a variety of small group and large group activities?
- Help create a safe environment, with rules that protect people from emotional and physical bullying?
- Provide opportunities for personal successes in different areas of skill?
- Provide opportunities for people to practice communication skills, such as listening, empathizing, and expressing opinions.
- Clarify common values and, at the same time, recognize the diversity of certain values?
- Provide opportunities for people to take charge of their own lives?
- Structure opportunities for role-playing and empathizing to gain greater understanding of others?

- Provide opportunities for staff members to model the behaviors that promote a sense of community?
- Provide opportunities for people to choose and interact, within the limitations of the community structure?
- Facilitate the resolution of conflicts, rather than pretending that they don't exist?
- Provide opportunities for people to help each other and be helped?

SUMMARY

This completes our chapter on community-building activities. What is the thread that ties them all together? What are the common elements of activities that build a sense of community in people? These commonalities may be considered criteria for judging and developing community-building activities. Each of these activities is characterized by the following:

- Encourages total group interaction over a period of time
- Promotes attitudes of self- and group-worth and capability
- Has, as a goal, a worthwhile product or a sense of accomplishment
- Is appropriate to the age and interest level of the participants
- Allows individuals to contribute to the task or solution in their own unique way
- Has a high probability for the participants to experience a feeling of success
- Incorporates an inherent sense of excitement, adventure, or importance
- Has a built-in vehicle of cooperation and interdependence

All community-building activities could be analyzed, discussed, and processed after completion. The dynamics of each activity can be examined from the points of view of both the individual and the group. The ultimate test for a community-building activity is the question, "Do you feel better about yourself and more accepted by the group?" If the answer is "yes," then the activity is important in developing a sense of community.

> "The harmonizing of natural community with human community was an ongoing process in Indigenous education."
>
> —Gregory Cajete

GIVING CREDIT WHERE CREDIT IS DUE

Some activity ideas in this chapter were inspired by the book, *Cowtails & Cobras*, by Karl Rohnke, published in 1977 by Project Adventure in Hamilton, Massachusetts.

Among the ideas included are Trust Fall, All Aboard, Reach for the Sky, Happy Landings, Diminishing Load, The Four Pointer, Pyramid, and The Clock.

Rohnke revised this book in 1989 and titled it *Cowtails and Cobras II: A Guide to Games, Initiatives, Ropes Courses, & Adventure Curriculum* (Kendall/Hunt Publishing Company). The activity, Artist-Clay Model, came from a mimeographed paper from the Minnesota Outward Bound School. Blind Square originated in a paper by Jim Merritt of the New Jersey School of Conservation, Branchville, New Jersey.

For profound and practical insights about community building, we encourage you to see Chapters 5, 7, and 8 in our companion volume, *Humanizing Outdoor and Environmental Education*, which is described at the beginning of the Resources chapter in this book. Matt Weinstein and Jeff McKay share their experience and wisdom in building community. Chapter 9 in that book offers a detailed case study of the community in the Human Relations Youth Adventure Camp.

CHAPTER 5

TRAIL MARKERS: CLARIFYING PERSONAL, SOCIAL, AND ENVIRONMENTAL VALUES

dina_sidelnikov/iStock/Thinkstock

"The most important human endeavor is the striving for morality in our actions. Our inner balance and even our existence depend on it."

—Albert Einstein

Values serve as guideposts as we experience life. Our priorities and chosen lifestyle mirror our values. We see a need to ensure a connection between the outdoor and environmental education experience and the rest of the "real world." Values can be the bridge.

Schools, camps, youth groups, outdoor education programs, and parents are in an excellent position to make a difference with regard to helping students and campers develop value systems that are rewarding, both to the individual and to the society. Camps and outdoor programs offer natural environments for people to see, hear, and interact with each other as humans. In an atmosphere of mutual trust, openness, respect for diversity, a sense of wonder, and an excitement about learning, it may be possible to make great strides in examining issues that are often difficult in other settings. These are the very issues that are vital to our nation in the 21st Century, and are of interest and concern to both young people and adults:

aging	*justice*
authority	*leisure*
citizenship	*lifestyles*
climate change	*marriage*
consumerism	*money*
cyberbullying	*nuclear power*
drug abuse	*pollution*
energy alternatives	*poverty*
friendship	*racism*
gender roles	*technology*
honesty	*war/peace*
hunger	*work*
immigration	

If we intend to humanize schools, camping, and outdoor education programs, it is crucial that we legitimize and build in opportunities to focus on human concerns—and that we create opportunities for people to develop the valuing skills they will need to sort through these complex issues. These skills include the following seven criteria from the pioneering book, *Values and Teaching:*
- To choose freely in appropriate areas of life
- To choose with an awareness of the available alternatives
- To carefully examine the possible consequences of these alternatives
- To prize their choices
- To affirm their choices, either verbally or in writing, when appropriate
- To act upon their choices in day-to-day activities
- To act repeatedly over time in recognizable patterns

The key to realize is that the emphasis is on teaching valuing skills, and not on teaching values per se. Again, we refer to the passage, "If you give me a fish, I'll eat tonight. If you teach me how to fish, I'll eat for a lifetime." We're interested in promoting an effective, lifelong approach to working with values, rather than either the hit-and-run moralizing approach or the hit-and-miss laissez faire approach to working with values.

This chapter provides a wide variety of over 60 suggested activities to explore values issues and to develop valuing skills. These are not the only activities that could serve this purpose. As previously noted, you are also encouraged to create your own activities, to springboard off the ones offered, and to invite the participants in your program to generate ideas as well (we have found the participants in our programs to have a wealth of ideas and creativity).

LEADERSHIP TIPS: GUIDELINES FOR WORKING WITH VALUES

For teachers, camp staff, youth group leaders, counselors, and parents, we recommend that you first actually *do* the activities yourself, for as the old Chinese proverb says, "I hear, and I forget; I see, and I remember; I do, and I understand." Afterwards, in applying, adapting, or stretching these activities to fit the groups with whom you work, you might want to consider the following guidelines:

- Remember that participants have a right to pass—this guideline is crucial if we are to build a safe atmosphere, and if we are to respect the privacy of the individual. If at any point, a person chooses not to share his/her thoughts, all that needs to be said is, "I pass." We hope this guideline would be respected.
- Try to avoid the "right answer" syndrome—this guideline is important if we are to encourage individual creative thinking and to minimize peer pressure. The complexity of many values issues also suggests that there may not be any one "right answer" in the back of the book.
- Keep the focus on the positive and on supporting one another—this guideline is especially helpful in addressing issues that may carry strong emotions. We always call for a moratorium on put-downs during values discussions.

Never forget that the activities should be understood as a means, not an end, in the process of developing valuing skills. After opening up an area for values exploration, the leader can aid participants in honing their skills by asking clarifying questions.

The following is an example of the kinds of questions that can move people beyond the fun and excitement of the activities themselves:

- Where do you suppose you first got that idea?
- How long have you felt that way?
- What else did you consider before you picked this?
- Was it a hard decision? What went into the final decision?
- Is this what I understand you to say …?
- What will you have to do? What are your first steps?

- In what way would life be different without it?
- Is it something you really prize?
- Would you be willing to sign a petition supporting that idea?
- What are the consequences of your choice?
- Who has influenced your decision?
- Where will this lead you? How far are you willing to go?
- How has it already affected your life? How will it affect you in the future?
- Have you done anything about it? Do you do this often?
- Are you the only one in your crowd who feels this way?

There are three kinds of arenas in which these activities and clarifying questions can be employed:

- Time set aside specifically for values exploration and skill development (e.g., at a daily sharing session, as part of the evening campfire, at a staff training workshop, or during a one-day retreat)
- Integrated in the study of some other subject area (e.g., biology, social studies, or crafts)
- Spontaneously, when the opportunity arises. Camping and outdoor education programs, with a multitude of opportunities for people to live, work, and play together, offer numerous on-the-spot invitations to tackle values issues and to practice valuing skills. We just need to be on our toes, and seize the opportunities. Now, a chance for you to dig in ...

INDOOR ACTIVITIES

❑ Activity #98: Hand-Wave Voting

Changes in personal behavior sometimes occur after someone simply points out an inconsistency in your life. Just hearing another point of view is often enough to spur people to reflect on the way they think and act.

Hand-wave voting is a quick method to create awareness of issues that invite further thought. Read the following list of prepared questions slowly enough, so that you and the members of your group have a chance to indicate your position on each. If your response is positive, or you agree strongly, then wave your hand wildly in the air. If you are against the idea, or your response is negative, then wave your thumb rapidly in a lowered position. If you wish to pass on the question, or are undecided, then fold your arms. The movement of the hand up or down and back and forth gives some indication of the intensity of your feeling about each issue.

The following are sample questions for you to try—how many of you ...:
- Would like to add new activities to your camp program?
- Have slept in a tent for more than a week this year?

- Enjoy walking in the woods?
- Admire the teenagers of this generation for their good qualities?
- Think that camps should help people become clearer about their values in their life?
- Have changed your lifestyle in the past year to improve the environment?
- Have publicly taken a stand on an environmental issue?
- Can think of something you could do tomorrow to improve the environment?
- Have wondered about how long people will inhabit the earth?
- Save scrap paper for writing notes?
- Recycle glass? Aluminum? Paper?
- Turn out the lights when leaving the room to save energy?
- Pick up litter sometimes?
- Would encourage your parents to join carpools to save gasoline?
- Would want to improve the insulation in your home to save energy?
- Think the flow of people into crowded national parks should be controlled to preserve them?
- Think more governmental controls are needed to achieve environmental quality?
- Think less governmental controls are needed to achieve environmental quality?
- Feel that the profit motive of free enterprise is the major barrier to a cleaner environment?
- Believe in recycling and reusing resources?
- Feel that the schools can influence student behaviors leading to an improved environment?
- Would sign a petition today banning nuclear plants?
- Read newspaper or on-line articles concerning environmental issues regularly?
- Feel that writing a letter to someone about an environmental problem in your community can help to correct it?
- Think that as a group, elementary pupils are more interested in cleaning up the environment than adults?
- Believe that this planet is already overpopulated?
- Would rank environmental quality as this country's greatest concern?
- Believe that humans play a role in "climate change?"
- Would choose a car by considering its impact on air pollution?
- Think that federally-owned wilderness lands should be kept forever wild?
- Eat organically grown foods as part of your regular diet?
- Think that science and technology will produce enough food to feed the world's hungry population?
- Believe that the earth holds vast quantities of untapped natural resources?
- Think that human intelligence will overcome the dangers of global warming?
- Would like to ban all strip mining of coal in this country?
- Think that atomic energy is one answer to our future energy requirements?
- Think that solar energy and wind power can contribute to our future energy requirements?

- Think that fracking might be the cause of earthquakes?
- Feel that all hard pesticides should be banned despite their effectiveness for killing pests?

The list of voting questions that can be asked is unlimited. Participants are often interested in looking around at how others vote. The diversity of values often prompts spontaneous discussions, which, in turn, may motivate self-examination.

❑ Activity #99: Ten Things I Love to Do in Camp or School

This activity is a more private way for you to examine personal values in your camp, school, or family. Start by listing 10 things you love to do down the left side of a piece of paper. On the right side of the paper, draw six columns to help you examine your loves.

Next, in the first column, put a check by those items that are regularly scheduled activities during the day. In the second column, place an "A" if you like to do the activity *alone*, a " +1" if you like the activity with one other person, and a "P" if you prefer doing it with lots of *people*. In the third column, mark a "B" next to each item at which you would like to become better. The fourth column is where you can rank your top choices, from 1-5. In the fifth column, put an "O" next to those items you would like to do *often*. Finally, place a "T" in the last column next to those items you would like to teach others to do.

After doing the codings, you may find it helpful to analyze the data by completing "I learned ..." statements (see Activity #115: Learning Journal). You may also want to do this activity periodically to see if any changes occur over time. Of course, new codings can be used later to examine the same items in different ways.

Experience has shown that few people like to code more than six columns. In addition to the codings listed, you and your participants might consider these: the date to indicate when the activity was last done; "SA" for those activities enjoyed with people of the same *age*; "SE" for those activities that require special equipment; "W" for those done best in the *wilderness*; " +E" for those having a *positive effect* on the environment; and " –E" for those having a *negative effect* on the environment. Feel free to use your creativity in inventing more codings—and encourage your staff and participants to do the same.

❑ Activity #100: Environmental Continuum

A continuum is an excellent means for you to publicly state your positions on issues. Usually, continua are created that have unrealistic extremes at either end as a way of forcing you to stand somewhere in between. Also, the exact middle of the continuum is said to be off-limits in order to encourage you not to fence-sit.

There are a number of ways in which you can use the continuum. For example, it may be done individually on paper. Another option would be for you to draw a continuum on newsprint or on a blackboard, and then have people in the group place their initials on the continuum to represent where they stand. Another way is to create the extremes on either side of a room or outside. People could then physically place themselves in a position that represents their view. In this instance, they would be literally taking a stand.

Following are some continua to consider:

Use of Electricity:
Peter Power (lights flood lamps 24 hours a day) .... Carrie Candle (only uses candles for lighting)

Greenery:
Asphalt Arnie (covers the yard with asphalt) .... Flora Flora (grows plants on every square inch of property)

Littering:
Pam Pickup (picks up all litter at all times)....................... Tommy Toss (tosses litter on the ground for a living)

Transportation:
Audrey Auto (uses her car for everything— .... Freddy Foot (walks everywhere, including "walking" the dog) lets air out of tires of others' cars)

Recycling:
Reusable Roger (repairs paper... Throw-away Thea (after one cups with tape in order to reuse) use, throws away fine china)

Environmental Freedom of Choice:
Complete individual freedom .... Total environmental control

Gypsy Moth Invasion:
Spraying Steve (uses as many... Let 'em Be Bert (even if it costs poison sprays as he can find) you your prize tree)

Home Water Use:
Capture raindrops to save for drinking................................ Let water run for one hour before using

Watercraft on a Lake:
Motoring Melvin (unlimited size of motors)....................... No-Motor Mike (canoes and sailboats only)

Energy Sources:
Complete energy self-sufficiency.. Complete dependence on foreign energy sources

Participant Choice in Activities:

Total free choice of activities by participants...................... Total scheduling of activities
by staff

One other way you may want to use the continuum is by focusing on the difference between where you would *like* to be on an issue and how you are *likely* to act. You could make one mark above the line and one mark below the line to distinguish between the two. You may choose to set a goal for yourself, in order to close the gap between "likely" and "like." The continuum is also a good stimulus for you to consider the consequences and alternatives with regard to a particular issue. In addition, it might be intriguing for you to share your reasoning with someone who is near you on the line, as well as with someone who is on the other end of the line.

You might also want to use a series of continua to help people explore a particular values issue. For example, if you were focusing on "wildlife", you could use the following seven continua:

Predators, like hawks, should be destroyed....................... Predators, like hawks, should be
when they interfere with humans.   protected completely, even

There should be no restrictions on importing.................. No new foreign wildlife should
foreign wildlife to this country.   be imported to this country
                                                                for any reason.

Wildlife refuges should be open to hunting. .... Hunting should never be
                                                                permitted on wildlife refuges.

It doesn't matter at all to me, if an... It matters a great deal to me if
animal species becomes extinct.   an animal species were to
                                                                become extinct.

Wildlife is very important in my life...................................... Wildlife is not important at all
                                                                in my life.

The great bison herds should have .... It is not necessary to preserve
been preserved as they were   any bison.

I don't want to spend any time helping wildlife.............. I want to spend all of my free
                                                                time helping wild life.

Following are more examples of continua that you could use to help people clarify their values about "open space" issues:

Wetlands are worthless and should.................................... Wetlands are more valuable
be eliminated completely.   than any other type of open
                                                                land, and all of them must
                                                                be preserved.

Having open space is not important	Having open space is very
at all in my life.	important in my life.

I would never allow national parks to	I would be very willing to have
be developed for other purposes	the national parks developed
in the future.	for other purposes in the future.

Strip mining and fracking should not be	Strip mining and fracking should
subject to any governmental controls.	be banned completely
	everywhere in the country.

❑ Activity #101: Button, Button, Who's Got the Button?

Pin-on buttons, with slogans or messages about the environment or other issues, have been popular over the years. Take some time to design and make a button that expresses a values position about the environment. Pick an issue about which you feel strongly. This activity is your chance to use a visual technique to create awareness about a particular environmental cause. For example, some causes about which people can have strong feelings include: protecting endangered species; banning of fracking and strip mining; dismantling nuclear plants; reducing air pollution; stopping clear-cutting of trees; and slowing global warming.

For this activity, provide crayons, magic markers, pieces of oak tag or cardboard, scissors, and different-sized objects for tracing circles. Note the variety of shapes and sizes of the buttons being made. When the buttons are completed, tape them to your clothing and share them with others.

To modify this activity, make bumper stickers, picket signs, or sandwich boards to state your concern. An environmental parade on the order of the original Earth Day can be organized. Floats and decorations may follow, if you and the participants want to create a bigger production, using this idea.

❑ Activity #102: Environmental Petition

As a follow-up to the "Button" activity, you, staff, and participants in your program can write a petition and then pass it around to gather signatures. The act of signing your name to a piece of paper is not only a clarifying experience, but also an opportunity for you to make a commitment to changing behavior and doing more about an issue. Consider some of these questions: How freely do you sign your name to different petitions? Do you ever refuse to sign until you study the issue more thoroughly? When are enough facts present for you to take a stand on an issue? Is it okay to change your mind on an issue when new information is received? Petition writing and signing can be fun, as well as a means to institute change.

❑ Activity #103: Environmental Geography

This activity is designed to encourage both physical and mental movement. Describe an imaginary map using the walls in a room or other objects outside. The map can be of the United States, a particular state, a continent, or the world. Direct people to move to the area of the imaginary map that fits the appropriate question. For example, go to the location on the map where you …

- Were born.
- Would like to take a vacation.
- Would like to live when you retire.
- Think you would find the most breathtaking scenery.
- Would least like to live.
- Have experienced wilderness.
- Would find the city you most want to visit.
- Would like to swim or wade in the water.
- Think you would find the most excitement.
- Think you would find the most pollution.

Periodically, you can encourage people to discuss their opinions with those individuals around them. This activity is a good one to break the ice with a new group, as well as to learn more about people who have been together for a while.

❑ Activity #104: Partner Sharing

People like to share their values about many environmental issues, especially when they feel safe. One crucial ingredient of safety is to feel "listened to." It is important to reinforce good listening habits, when staff and participants are sharing with one another. It is vital for us to listen with our whole body, because body language usually speaks louder than words. There is nothing more satisfying than to be listened to and to be heard, when you have something to say about which you feel strongly.

This activity provides an arena for practicing listening skills, while talking about topics of interest and concern. In a group, have people form pairs for a five-minute period (this time can be extended as the participants' listening skills increase). Each partner then takes two and one-half minutes of uninterrupted airtime to talk about such topics as:

- When you say that you are for clean air or clean water, what do you really mean? How clean is clean?
- Find out what your partner would be willing to pay to reduce smog by 50 percent. Find out how much your partner is willing to pay to reduce other forms of pollution.
- Tell your partner as many things as you can about what you do to maintain a quality environment. In what areas could you do better?
- Do you think that the billions of dollars spent in the space program have been worth it? Has the space program made life on earth any better? How? Do you think there is a danger of polluting outer space? What could be done about this?

- You have just received a federal grant for a million dollars. How would you spend it to improve the quality of the environment?
- What appliances do you use in your home that consume relatively large amounts of electricity? Which ones could you eliminate or reduce the use of?
- Daniel Boone felt crowded when he could smell smoke from a neighbor's fire. When do you feel crowded? What makes a crowd for you?

❏ Activity #105: Environmental Auction

Auctions are not only fun, they also reveal a great deal about what you value. Conduct an auction using the following rules: you are to pretend that no one owns the items to be auctioned; you have a total of $50,000 to spend; you cannot spend more than $10,000 on any one item; and bids must open at no less than $100 and no more than $500 for each item.

The audience should keep a record of the amount of money they have before each item comes up for sale, the highest amount bid on each item, and their own bids. This information can be used to draw conclusions about their values after the auction. The following are examples of personal-use items that could be auctioned:

- A solar-powered vehicle
- A self-driving electric car
- Your home heated for a year with heat from the center of the earth
- A wind-driven generator to supply electricity to your home for a year
- Food containers that are biodegradable
- Twenty acres of forest land
- A garbage-burning furnace run on cheap and abundant fuel
- A private well for your house

Examples of items that you could share with others include the following:
- The power to save endangered animals
- Elimination of world hunger
- Reduction of air pollution
- Reduction of effects of global warming
- Clean water for swimming and drinking
- A steady world population
- A cheap way to get fresh water from the oceans
- A wilderness to stay wild forever

❏ Activity #106: Getting Acquainted With the Human Environment

At first glance, the purpose of this activity seems to enable people to meet each other. However, there is also a strong emphasis on values, as individuals consider some of the items on the list. Some people who have tried this activity seem to enjoy guessing which item may belong to another person.

Give a copy of the following list to each participant in the group. Feel free to change the directions or any of the items in order to fit your particular group.

Directions: After each item, fill in the name or names of people who fit each description. Try to talk with as many people in the group as possible. If you would like to talk with someone later, tell that person you have some "unfinished business." Use each person's name only once.

Find someone who:
- Signed a petition expressing a viewpoint on an environmental issue.
- Feeds birds during winter.
- Has changed their lifestyle in the last year to improve the environment.
- Maintains a compost pile.
- Gets more than 25 miles to the gallon of gas in their vehicle.
- Has slept out under the stars recently.
- Has seen the sunrise within the past year.
- Was raised on a farm.
- Has been a city dweller forever.
- Rides a bicycle to work or school.
- Finds peace and relaxation in the wilderness.
- Has flown a kite within the last three years.
- Has never been to a nature center before.
- Likes to walk barefooted through the grass.
- Has caught a fish over 12-inches long.
- Enjoys the smell of soil.
- Likes to grow plants.
- Has cared for an injured wild animal.

❏ Activity #107: Environmental Impact

All humans and other living things make an impact on the environment, as they live and carry out life processes. It is impossible to live without making an environmental impact, but it is very possible to control the amount and kind of impact you may have. This activity asks you to look carefully at your daily lifestyle and to decide how it affects a quality world. Draw a line down the middle of a sheet of paper, making two columns. Head the first column with "Life Support Needs" and the second with "Luxury Desires." Fill in as many items as possible under each heading. After examining the lists, do you see any areas for change in your lifestyle? Check with others on this too.

❏ Activity #108: All My Life's a Circle

Another way to visualize environmental impact is to represent a typical day in your life with a circle. Divide the circle into slices proportionate in size to the specific ways in which you make an impact on the environment. For example, if you ride in a car for one hour a day, make a thin slice about 1/24 of the circle and label it "car rides." If you watch television for two hours each day, make a slice about 1/12 of the circle and label it "TV." If you use a computer or cell phone for three hours a day, carve out a slice for 1/8 of the circle. It might be interesting for you to color the "negative" influences red and the "positive" influences green. How do you draw the line between "positive" and "negative" influences? Compare a typical day at home with a typical day at camp or school. Which location shows a greater impact on the environment?

❑ Activity #109: Electric Grid

Still another way to examine your impact on the environment is to list all items you use that consume electricity. After doing this, code the items in the following ways: put a "P" after those items that provide *pleasure*; place a "C" next to those items that are *conveniences*; mark a "W" after items that are used while doing necessary *work*; put "BN" after those that you consider to be *basic needs*; place a "D" after items that you use *daily*; an "O" for those used *occasionally*, and an "R" for those items used *rarely*. It may be very revealing to compare your lifestyles in your program setting with those at home. How could the lifestyles in your program be simplified even more?

❑ Activity #110: Picture This

Spin-offs of the last three activities could involve creative role-playing in groups. Ask group members to draw a picture of a person who leads the most ecologically sound lifestyle—a person who makes the least negative impact on the environment. This activity provides much enjoyment, as the participants consider such things as how the person is to be dressed, what the person is doing for fun or work, and what that person uses for transportation. In addition to drawing the most ecologically sound person, a montage can be developed from magazine clippings to show how each person presently makes an impact on the environment, and another one showing how each person wishes to be. These activities are one way of moving from awareness to action with regard to environmental impact.

❑ Activity #111: Environmental Survey

This strategy offers a structure for you to capture your observations about the environment. After filling out the following survey form, you might want to discuss the items from a values perspective:

- The most numerous objects in view are _____.
- The most powerful force in the environment is _____.
- Something that I would like to add to this environment is _____.
- This environment is similar to (an animal) because _____.
- The funniest thing I see around is _____.
- This environment makes me feel _____.
- The most predictable thing about this environment is _____.

- If I could plan an ideal environment, it would include _____.
- Something I would change in the environment to make it better is _____ .

As noted at the beginning of this section, the purpose of these activities is to invite you, staff, and program participants to use indoor activities to explore your values—and to value the environment.

❑ Activity #112: Defuzzing Wheel

Many values-loaded words are fuzzy concepts—they mean many things to different people. In order to become aware of and explicit about your own definitions, thoughts, feelings, and associations around values-rich issues, we invite you to use the defuzzing wheel ... "Ride on!"

To start your ride, draw a circle with spokes coming out from it. Place the word or concept to be defuzzed (e.g., "nature") in the center of the circle. Next, freely associate to this concept by placing any thoughts, feelings, behaviors, individuals, conditions, etc. on the spokes leading out from the circle. Please feel free to jot down anything that comes to your mind, e.g., individual words, phrases, complete sentences, pictures. It is important for you not to censor or prejudge any of your ideas—there is no right answer to this.

The defuzzing wheel is an incredibly flexible vehicle. For instance, you could place in the center of the defuzzing wheel such fuzzy concepts that have multiple meanings as: competition, wise use of resources, drug abuse, citizenship, sexism, racism, global warming, good camp, good school, ideal camper, etc. It is an excellent way to open up an area for exploration and conversation.

❑ Activity #113: Think and Listen

After completing your wheel, you might find it helpful to join with one or more people to share your ideas. If one of your partners has an association with which you agree (but you initially did not include it on your wheel), go ahead and add it to yours. Avoid arguments over "who has the best wheel" or over specific ideas. The intent of this sharing is to expand your thinking repertoire and to encourage peer teaching. We have found it helpful to have each person, in turn, be the "focus person." In other words, participants have a specified amount of uninterrupted airtime to share ideas from their defuzzing wheels.

❑ Activity #114: Prioritizing

Of all the data now on your defuzzing wheel (your original wheel, plus the added ideas from your partners), what stands out the most for you? Which spoke of your wheel seems to get at the heart of the concept; which association seems to cover the most ground? Place an asterisk next to that spoke, and note (either in your mind and/or on paper) what makes that association the most significant one for you.

❑ Activity #115: Whip-Around

Whip-Around provides a chance for you to share a great deal of significant data with others in a relatively short time. Seat yourselves so that everyone can see everyone else's face (circular seating—in a classroom or around a campfire—seems to facilitate this). Announce the "theme" of the whip-around (e.g., the priorities from your defuzzing wheels, something that you appreciate about others in the group, etc.). Then, each person who wants a turn can briefly respond to the topic. In using a whip-around to follow-up the defuzzing wheel, we have often found it helpful to record the ideas generated on a blackboard, whiteboard, or newsprint. This can lead to identifying the major themes on which the group would like to focus in addressing a particular topic. This is also one way of developing a program around the interests and priorities of the participants.

❑ Activity #116: Learning Journal

This activity is a chance for you to reflect on what you have learned through a written log. Complete the following kinds of statements:
- I learned that I …
- I relearned that I …
- I noticed that I …

- I became aware that I …
- I was pleased that I …
- I was surprised that I …
- I hope that I …
- I will …
- I want to learn more about …
- The strongest feeling I have is …
- With regard to the topic we are discussing, I appreciate the fact that I …

❑ Activity #117: Values Metaphor Hunt

Nature abounds with metaphors for values issues. One way for you to tap this metaphorical gold mine is for you to think of examples of the values issues you face in the world of nature (or in your local community, if that is your immediate environment). To do this, go on a "scavenger hunt in your mind," and locate things to complete the following: _____ from the world of nature is like (or reminds me of) *the values issue at hand*. For instance, if citizenship is the issue at hand, you might have a metaphor hunt inventory that would include: a hive of bees, a colony of ants, the eagle, etc. This activity is a way of physicalizing the defuzzing wheel. You could certainly follow it up with Activities #113 to 116.

❑ Activity #118: The Sense of Wonder

There are, indeed, at least eight senses. In addition to sight, sound, touch, smell, and taste, we have the sense of place, sense of wonder, and the sense of humor. And it makes a great deal of *sense* that *wonder* is at the heart of all learning. One way of discovering how wonder-full you are is to complete the following sentence stem: "With regard to *the values issue at hand*, I wonder …" You can use these wonderings to keep you from wandering. These wonderings can serve as the guideposts for you to focus on the particular values area.

Some examples of wonderings generated by teenagers include the following:
- With regard to racism, I wonder: What stereotypes people have; how to reduce suspicion; how to avoid prejudices; how I can be proud of my heritage, without being subject to attack; how we can make people more sensitive to the impact of racism; if the younger generation is any less racist than the older; if a war could break out due to racism in the near future.
- With regard to sexism and gender roles, I wonder: How to bring it to a personal level, and not to a national level; what I can do at home and school to confront sexism; what kinds of fears other people have; how to break sexism handed down by parents; if it is greater in some geographical areas than others; how I can recognize sexism; what the role of trust is in a meaningful relationship.

- With regard to work, I wonder: If I should have some direction in vocation before college; what it would be like to work for myself, not someone else; why some work becomes monotonous and less self-satisfying; what my cutoff is between work and pleasure; if I will have to compromise myself by doing work I don't like in order to support myself or my family; why I feel I'll never be content with one occupation for my life but will try many; how to work to live, not live to work.
- With regard to war, I wonder: Why it exists; whether I or anybody else should be forced to support war; if war will always be a part of us; if there are any feasible alternatives; if I am against all wars; why people feel it is necessary to kill others; if ideas and money are as important as human life.
- With regard to family and lifestyles, I wonder: If I can be open with my relatives when I haven't been especially open up to now; why I don't show more appreciation to my family; if it is okay to have a family, given the world population situation; what will become of my family when I leave home; what role children should play in the family; how I can get back with my family; how much a family should demand conformity to one lifestyle.
- With regard to drugs, I wonder: If drugs are really a cop-out or just an occasional pleasure trip; how to resolve the inconsistency between believing in my body and mind being directed by myself and my liking to do some drugs; how to relate to people who do drugs when I don't do them myself; why I first tried drugs; why people make something as unstable as drugs a crutch.
- With regard to money, I wonder: How it can best be used; how I can give up some for others who don't have as much as me; if I can get everything I want from life without it; how much I will sacrifice for money; why it destroys so much; why I think of it as a means to an end instead of a real goal in itself; how important it is to feel successful.

❏ Activity #119: Think-and-Listen-to-Yourself Solo

Any one of the wonderings mentioned in the previous activity, or any of the wonderings you generated for yourself, could lead into a full values exploration unit. This activity provides a structure for questioning and thinking to yourself.

Survey your immediate environment. Find a spot where you will be alone, undisturbed, and peaceful for a period of time. Using a journal, jot down significant questions and thoughts you have with regard to one of the values areas. Interview yourself, using nonjudgmental clarifying questions. This activity is one way of recognizing and tapping your own resources. When you return from the solo, you might choose to join with others and share through a think-and-listen format or through a whip-around.

❑ Activity #120: You are Resource-Full

Purestock/Thinkstock

Not only are you wonderful and wonder-full, you are also resource-full. Furthermore, so are the people around you—both the staff and the participants in your program. This activity is an opportunity for you to build on these resources while also tackling important social values issues. Take a look at the following list of people:

- Ms. Lee Sure: An expert in helping you to use your leisure time in the most enjoyable ways. She is sure to relax you and fill your life with fun.

- Dr. Santa Tation: Guarantees a pollution-free life for you. An advocate of "clean living," he will ensure that you use intelligent means of waste disposal and that your environment is free of air and water pollution.

- Noah T. All: Has an incredible reservoir of knowledge that he can give you. He can help you in becoming a walking encyclopedia, with intelligent ideas always at your fingertips and on the tip of your tongue.

- Dr. N. R. Gee: Is a bundle of excitement. She can transfer to you a delight-full ability to energize those around you. As an energy source, you will have a magnetic personality that draws people to you.

- Bill D. Body: An outstanding athlete, Bill can help you develop your physical capacities and will guarantee that you will be in shape for the rest of your life.

- Prof. Hugh Manistic: Is a very compassionate, caring, and understanding individual. He has the ability to help you become incredibly empathic and comforting—someone whom people feel free to turn to in times of stress and distress.

- Dr. Neural Plural: Has the amazing trait of being completely open-minded. She never puts down anyone or any idea and has the nifty ability to accept and see the worth of different people, ideas, and lifestyles.

- G. Clef: An outstanding musician, Ms. Clef can help you develop your musical talents to the nth degree. She can also aid you in your growing appreciation of the arts to the point where you could be termed a connoisseur.

- Warren Peace: A renowned authority on conflict resolution, Warren can guarantee that your personal life will be a peaceful one. He also will make sure that your environment will be filled with harmony.
- Connie Sumer: An expert in consumer affairs, Connie will guarantee that you will make wise choices in the purchase and use of materials and services. You will never have any hassles with stores, and you will never be "ripped off."

This list of resource people can be used in the following ways: in your journal, write down whom each of these people reminds you of—this could be a chance for you to identify the resources of your family, friends, staff, and participants in your program; place a "+" next to three of the names—these would be the people who remind you of skills that you have (allow yourself the luxury of bragging for just a moment, for instance, if you see yourself as enthusiastic, you might put a "+" next to Dr. N. R. Gee); place a "+" next to three of the names—these would be the people who have skills that you would like more of in your own life; rank these people from 1 to 10, as if they were applying for a job in your program: your ranking will reflect what you value; if you want a real challenge, join together with a group of five other people (staff and/ or participants), and try to reach consensus on your rankings. By consensus, we mean that everyone would agree with the group's decision, and would be willing to publicly affirm it. In other words, consensus does not mean "voting," "railroading," or "taking an average of the rankings"; and feel free to add (or to have staff and participants add) to the list of people. It might be fun for you to create your own list. Think of ways you could adapt this activity for the participants in the program—e.g., rank-order your preferences for whom you would like as a cabin mate, or as a counselor.

❏ Activity #121: Moral Dilemma Story

Each of us faces moral dilemmas every day of our lives. The following is an example of one story that you can use as a vehicle to clarify your values, with regard to social issues:

> *Once upon a time, there was a school called American High. Bill, an African-American junior, wanted to set up an African-American folklore program on Monday afternoons during the first semester. This was the best time for the 15 Black students who were interested in the course, and also the only time that Bill's outside resource people could be of help. Since they hoped to show videos during the course, the students needed to use the school's audiovisual room (which has only one LCD projector).*
>
> *Bill approached the vice principal, explained his course, and asked to be able to use the A-V room every Monday afternoon for the semester. The vice principal okayed the program, and gave permission for use of the room.*
>
> *The following Monday, Bill and the other 14 Black students arrived at the A-V room after school, only to find it occupied by the players on the football team, who were watching their game film from Saturday.*

The 45 football players and coaches refused to leave the room, even after Bill explained that he had permission from the vice principal. In fact, Art, one of the players, blurted out, "Why don't you *explitive-deleted* wait until the end of football season to have your course—football is more important to this school than studying about artsy-craftsy junk and stories about *racial epithet*."

Tempers flared, and a big argument ensued. Ernie, another football player, felt strongly that the Black students should have first priority to the room, and was appalled by Art's outburst. But, Ernie did not say anything at all.

Bill charged back to the vice principal. After hearing of the conflict, however, the vice principal rescinded permission for use of the A-V room. His reasons included the following: 45 students is more than 15—we have to respect the rights of the greater number; the football team provides a service for the school—your course would not; you can postpone your course and have it next semester.

A week rolled by, and next Monday afternoon came up. It found Bill and his 14 Black friends occupying the A-V room, and not letting anyone in. Bill told the football team that his course would be using the room for the rest of the semester. Upon hearing this, John, one of the football players, proceeded to break into and steal from some of the Black students' school lockers. John felt that "some of my best friends are Black, but those people occupying the room are being insensitive and destructive."

Are you ready for the next step? Try to rank-order five characters in the story from the one whose *behavior* you consider to be most humane to the one whose *behavior* you consider to be least humane (in other words, we are asking you to make a value-decision on their actions, and not on their worth as people). Jot down the criteria you used in making this decision. Next, if you are brave, you could join up with four other people and try to reach consensus on your rankings. At the end of the discussion, it might be helpful to identify and summarize the major value issues around which the decisions were based.

The following are some of the values criteria that one group of young people considered in seeking consensus:
- Responsibility, taking the initiative (Bill)
- Going through proper channels (Bill)
- Use of racial slurs (Art)
- Speaking out on one's convictions and beliefs (Ernie)
- Courage, decisiveness, considering alternatives (vice principal)
- Violence against material goods (John)

- Violence against people—physical and non-physical
- Who could have acted differently to prevent this from happening? Who was in the best position to avoid and/or deal with the conflict?
- Whose behavior caused the most hurt to people? In the short-run? In the long-run?

Finally, you might want to consider the following questions (in your journal and/or with the people in your consensus group):

- Would your ranking have been changed if Bill's group had been a branch of the Sierra Club (rather an African-American folklore group)? What if the group was focusing on women's studies? What if the group was a politically-oriented, anti-nuclear power one? What if the group was an ecology club that was interested in performing service projects for the school? As you can see, these questions provide insight into ways that you could change the moral dilemma story to focus on other values areas.
- How did you and your group operate in the consensus discussion, as compared with your performance in the consensus discussion Activity #119? It is not often that we have a "second chance to go around in life" … what goals do you set for yourself in future group discussions (whether it be with staff or participants in your program)? What can you do to provide more effective leadership in the task groups of which you are a part?

Keep your eyes open to "real-life" moral dilemmas that occur in your program or school. Tapping them is an excellent way to help people practice skills in considering consequences, generating alternatives, listening to others, and respecting differences.

❑ Activity #122: Values Sheets

The formula for this activity is simple: all you need is a provocative stimulus (an object from nature, an excerpt from a book or magazine or online story, an item from the newspaper, a song, a movie, etc.), followed by a series of clarifying questions—questions that will help you examine how the stimulus relates to you, your personal life, your values. After individually reading the stimulus and completing the follow-up questions on a values sheet, you can join with others to compare notes and reactions. Here are several thought-provoking values sheets designed to get your wheels turning:

<u>Values Sheet "A": Dead or Alive</u>

"The wise, old hermit lived in the woods outside a small Midwestern town. The wisdom of this man was widely known throughout the community. Many of the young men in the town spent a good deal of their time trying to disprove his wisdom, so that all of the world would know "he's not so smart after all."

One day, two young men sitting on the bank of the river were indulging in their favorite sport … looking for a way to trick the hermit and thus end the legend of his wisdom. Suddenly, one of the young men reached out and trapped a sparrow that had perched on the limb above his head. "I know how we can out-fox the hermit," he said.

"We'll go to the hermit's cave, and I'll hide the sparrow cupped in my hand so he can't see it. I'll ask him, 'What have I in my hands?' If he is able to tell me that it is a bird, I'll then ask him, 'Is it dead or alive?' If he says it is alive, I'll squash my hands, and the bird will be dead. If he says it's dead, I'll open my hands and let the sparrow fly away." Hurrying through the woods, they soon came to the hermit's cave.

"Old man," cried the tormentor, 'what have I in my hands?" The old man looked at him thoughtfully and then answered him, "A bird, my son."

"Tell me, old man, is it dead or alive?" For a long time, the old man just looked at the boys, then answered, very slowly, very deliberately, "It's up to you, my son, it's in your hands."

Clarifying Questions to Think and Write On:

- Have you ever tried to prove that someone was not as smart as people said they were? If so, how did you do it? How did you feel afterwards?
- Would you try this same experiment with a bird in your hand? If the hermit had answered that the bird was alive, could you have crushed it to death? Have you ever killed a bird? A fish? Or other small animal? How did you feel then? How would you feel now? Have you changed?
- Do you consider hunting a sport for you? Does the answer to this question depend upon what animal is being hunted? Is hunting the protected whooping crane the same as hunting the more abundant white-tailed deer?
- How much power do you think you have in your hands, when it comes to protecting wildlife or saving open space from development? Have you ever done anything to accomplish these goals?

Values Sheet "B": Where Have All the Buffaloes Gone?

Directions: Read the quote and answer the questions in writing. There are no right or wrong answers to these values questions.

> "The buffalo is gone, and of all his millions, nothing is left but bones … The wolves that howled at evening about the traveler's campfire have succumbed to arsenic and hushed their savage music … The rattlesnakes have grown bashful and retiring. The mountain lion shrinks from the face of man, and even grim 'Old Ephraim," the grizzly bear, seeks the seclusion of his dens and caverns."
>
> —Francis Parkman, 1892

Clarifying Questions to Think and Write On:

- As long ago as 1892, people noticed that some wildlife were vanishing. Have you thought much about rare and endangered animals? Would it *really* make a big difference in your life if one of these animals became extinct because of humans?

- Do you think that Parkman is sorry to see that buffalo, wolves, rattlesnakes, mountain lions, and grizzly bears were disappearing? What words led you to believe how he felt about them?
- If you were to give advice to wildlife about how they could best co-exist with humans, what would you advise them? If you were to give advice to humans on how we could best co-exist with wildlife, what would you tell us?

Values Sheet "C": The Vermiculite Controversy

Directions: Read the following statement and answer the questions in writing. There are no right or wrong answers to these values questions.

A volcano erupted millions of years ago in Louisa County, Virginia. The volcano left a small 14,000-acre pocket of a mineral beneath the surface called vermiculite. Vermiculite comes from the Latin word "vermis" meaning worm. When the mineral is heated, it expands into wormlike shapes. It is used for cat litter, in insulation products, in concrete, and in agricultural soil conditioners. The big issue in Louisa County is whether to mine the vermiculite deposits or not. There are people on both sides of the controversy. There are strong reasons to support each side. Among the pros and cons are the following:

Pro Mining:

- Some landowners want their land mined so that they can make money.
- The mines would attract industry, create new jobs, and raise the tax base in the county.
- Vermiculite is a very useful product.
- It is wasteful not to use the vermiculite by developing the area. Progress must come, if the people are to raise their standard of living.
- The board of supervisors voted five to one to rezone the area to allow mining and changed the county ordinance to allow mining almost anywhere, no matter what the zoning.

Con Mining:

- The United States Department of the Interior declared the area a National Historic Landmark because of the colonial architecture.
- The mining would change the land by digging 10-acre pits up to 75-feet deep. Roads, settling ponds, and dumps would have to be built. Over 400 acres of land would be changed.
- The land was zoned for agriculture, not for mining, for many years.
- The Department of the Interior believes that the mining operation would harm the scenery of the area.
- Some landowners want to preserve the "unspoiled" and historical values of the land.

<u>Clarifying Questions to Think and Write On:</u>

What other pros and cons can you think of? Do you think the area should be mined? If you owned land in the area and could become rich by mining the vermiculite, would you sell or lease your land? Would you vote to change the zoning from agriculture to mining use? Who should have the say in how the land is used, the local people or the federal government?

<u>Values Sheet "D": John Muir—A Person Close to Nature</u>

Directions: Read the statements below and answer the questions in writing. There are no right or wrong answers to these values questions.

- John Muir was happiest when he could share his love of nature with others. What is something that makes you happy when you share it?
- John Muir collected plants and flowers and pressed them between two pieces of wood. Do you collect anything? If so, what?
- When John Muir was a boy in Scotland, he decided that disobeying his parents and going to an old castle was more important to him than staying home and playing in his yard. Have you ever felt so strongly about something that you broke a rule?
- John Muir won a prize for his inventions. He invented a machine to wake him up that told time, rang a bell in the morning, and even shook his bed. He also made a thermometer as tall as himself. He made a desk that opened and closed books so he could read faster. What is something you would like to invent? How would it be useful?
- When John Muir was a young man, he was blinded by pieces of flying metal while working in a factory, making wagon wheels. John was blind for many weeks. When he was able to see again, he believed that he had been given a second chance to see all the trees and flowers he had read about. If you knew you were going to lose your sight next week, what would you want to look at carefully so you could remember it?
- John Muir walked from Indiana to Florida, with only a few clothes and a compass, collecting plants along the way. Have you ever felt so strongly about something that you would walk many miles for it? What was it?
- When John Muir walked from Indiana to Florida, he said, "I am wild and free again!" What is something that you like to do that makes you feel wild and free?
- John Muir lived in a place called Yosemite Valley. A famous scientist said that the valley was made by great earthquakes. John Muir said that it was made by glaciers. The scientist laughed at Muir. A few years later, Muir found evidence that the valley was really formed by glaciers. Have you ever had someone laugh at you, because he thought you were wrong? How did it feel?
- John Muir and his friends formed the Sierra Club to help save wild places. Have you ever belonged to a club or organization? What were some of your reasons for joining?
- John Muir wrote, "We are all part of the wilderness, and the wilderness is part of us." How much of your thoughts and travels are related to the wilderness?

Values Sheet "E": Values and Actions

"They came for the Panthers, and I said nothing because I was not a Panther. They came for the Black man and I said nothing because I was not Black. Then they came for the students and I said nothing because I was not a student. Then they came for the liberals and I said nothing because I was not a liberal. And when they came for me, I looked around and said nothing, because I was alone."

—Elaine Brown

Clarifying Questions to Think and Write On:

- Do you identify with any of these people or categories?
- What are some things going on in your world right now about which you would like to speak up?
- Just how does one go about "speaking up?" Which ways are the most comfortable for you? The most effective? What advice would you give to the Ernies (see Activity #120) of the world to move from bystander to upstander?
- But why stick your neck out? Why not?
- When was the first time you "spoke up" against a racist, sexist, ethnic put-down joke? If you are unable to do it, who should?
- Would you use a few moments of silence to work out a plan by which you could, indeed, speak up about something important to you?
- If you could send an e-mail or text message to the director of this program about an important issue to you, what would you say?
- Some people say: "We need to speak up about and stand up for our values." Do you agree? If so, could you relate something you have done about something you valued?*

Values Sheet "F": Change

"Ills exist in society. Victims press for change. Or perhaps the advantaged person feels guilty and feels things should be changed. But change is difficult. Sometimes, it means changing habits or giving up some personal advantage, or just hard work. Part of us doesn't want to change. We may be content with merely expressing our concern, merely taking a picture of the problem, merely writing a report. But if someone is hungry, she will continue to be hungry. Social injustices do not go away just because we think about them."

Clarifying Questions to Think and Write On:

- What are your reactions to the aforementioned?
- Do you see yourself as doing something about some of the ills of society? What? When?
- Do you believe that "if you're not part of the solution, you're part of the problem?"

- What could others do to support you, if you were to try to change a habit? What habit would you like to experiment with giving up? What habit would be hardest for you to give up?
- Write a dialogue (or role play it) between the part of you that wants to change and the part of you that prefers not to change.
- Do you see any injustices in your school or camp? If so, what might you do about them?

Values Sheet "G": Dream Building

When a man starts out to build a world,
He starts first with himself …
Then, the mind starts seeking a way.
Then, the hand seeks other hands to help …
Thus, the dream becomes not one man's dream
But a community dream …
Not my world alone,
But your world and my world,
Belonging to all the hands who build.

—Langston Hughes

Clarifying Questions to Think On:

- What is something that you have "started out to build" in your own life?
- What ways have you found to be effective in "inviting" others to share your dream?
- Are there any dreams that you now have that you would like the staff and/or participants of this program to share and join?
- Do you have any ideas about how to build a better sense of "community" in this program?
- Martin Luther King had a dream, which he unfortunately did not live to see fulfilled. What dreams do you want to realize in your lifetime?

Values Sheet "H": Conflict

"Beetles don't argue with butterflies."

Clarifying Questions to Think On:

- What does the quote mean to you?
- Where have you experienced or observed conflict in your life? What conflicts have you noted in this program?
- How do you usually handle conflict situations? When you are a participant? When you are an "outsider?"

- What is your reaction to the statement: "Without conflict, we cannot grow."?
- What guidelines have you used in resolving conflicts in your own life that our nation might want to apply? If you were to send a telegram to the President with your recommendations, what would you say?
- Which of the following describes how you usually deal with conflict? Which would you like to have describe you? If there's a gap between what you're *likely* to do and what you'd *like* to do, what can you do to close the gap?. In that regard, you could: avoid conflict at all costs; negotiate; engage in nonviolent direct action; use physical force; withdraw from conflict; give in; stand firm, not budge.
- What recommendations do you have for resolving conflicts in this program?
- What other examples from the world of nature can you find that illustrate conflict or the lack of conflict?

❑ Activity #123: Bill of Rights Revisited

The Bill of Rights lies at the heart of our nation's values around liberty, justice, and the pursuit of happiness. Ironically, as reflected in several recent studies, this document would probably be rejected by Americans, if it were put to a vote today. This activity uses the Bill of Rights to help you clarify your values related to social issues.

First, try ranking the 10 amendments in the order of their personal importance to you. You might also want to rank them according to which rights seem closest to being abridged today and which are most secure. With regard to your own program, which rights are most important—this might suggest another ranking for you to do.

It might also be intriguing to join with staff and/or participants to discuss or seek consensus on these rankings. In addition, you could take some time to reflect on how you might expand the Bill of Rights. What other "rights" do you think are crucial to people in our country? In the world? In your program?

For your interest, the following are some "rights" generated by a group of elementary school students:
- Right to more field trips, since "we would learn more and understand more of our studies by seeing the things that we are studying"
- Right to play sports with mixed teams (boy-girl)
- Right to one's own thoughts
- Right to eat—being able to choose among cafeteria foods
- Right to earn money by working
- Right to privacy, being alone when one wants
- Right to one's own feelings—"nobody can tell you how to feel"

Similarly, a group of high school students suggested the following rights:
- Right to a good education
- Right to be responsible

- Right to be able to distribute political literature
- Right to voice opinions with no penalty
- Right to evaluate staff
- Right to express oneself emotionally
- Right to freedom of learning
- Right to be seen as human
- Right to not be put in a category
- Right to dress as one wants
- Right to have staff have confidence in us.

This particular activity can help you, staff, and participants in your program to establish a just community, based upon a mutual understanding of one another's rights and responsibilities. At the same time, this activity could serve as a microcosm for creating a just "world community" and for negotiating the attendant values issues.

It might be interesting for you to take an inventory of the rights/rules/laws of nature. What parallels do you see between these and human rights/rules/laws? What "rights of the natural environment" do you want to preserve/protect in the rules of your program? Perhaps, you could title your list as "Ecological Bill of Rights."

❑ Activity #124: Action Research + Action Search

This strategy is designed to help you act on your good intentions. Start by listing examples of injustices, oppression, and/or violations of your or your program's bill of rights. For instance, you might come up with such items as:
- Textbooks that exclude or distort minority contributions to America
- Hiring standards for camping programs that are culturally biased
- Forbidding girls to play in sports leagues
- Pollution of streams by local industry
- People who consistently tell ethnic jokes
- People who constantly litter

Next,it is time to search for actions to speak to the problems that your research has uncovered. Taking one problem at a time, brainstorm what you can do to address it. First, a word about "brainstorming," which is probably one of the most frequently mentioned and oft-misused techniques for generating alternative solutions. What we suggest is that if you fly with the DOVE, then your brainstorming sessions will also soar:
- D: Defer judgment—All ideas are acceptable; avoid killer statements like "That's stupid," "It'll never work, "People won't like you for that," etc.; take a positive focus on every idea that comes up (your ideas, as well as others' ideas); hold off on criticisms—don't "drive" with your brakes on.
- O: Off-beat—Try to generate as many weird, strange, different ideas as possible; use metaphors and analogies to help break out of traditional mental ruts; try to

make the familiar strange; off-beat ideas can lead to humor and laughter (HAHA!), which, in turn, can spark creative ideas (AHA!).

- V: Vast number—Seek as many ideas as you can; the more ideas, the better chance you have of finding good ideas; go for quantity—the quality check will come later.
- E: Expand—The object in brainstorming is to piggyback or hitchhike on your own ideas and on the ideas of others; try to build on the contributions of your peers; cooperation and synergy, rather than competition, are encouraged.

Following the DOVE guidelines, generate a list of possible solutions to the problem at hand. When you have your list, take a moment to analyze it by using the following coding: place a "T" next to those actions that you would feel comfortable/effective in *trying*; place a "C" next to those actions that you would *consider* pursuing; and put an "N" beside those behaviors that you would prefer *not* to try at this point in time.

In order to increase the probability of success in carrying out your good intentions, you may find it helpful to commit yourself to writing a contract with yourself (and/or with another person who could support you as you seek to implement your contract). The contract might include the following elements: completion of an "I will …" statement— worded to focus on action; specification of a date—to serve as a timeline for yourself; your signature; and your support partner's signature, along with the specific ways and timeline for your partner's support (if you extend your contract to another person).

The following are examples of possible contracts:

- I will write a letter to the local paper and to my representatives making them aware of the pollution caused by the local industries. I will write these letters by next Tuesday. Signed, Gail … I will support Gail by gently nudging her—I'll do this by kidding with her whenever I see her (like asking her if she's written her "smelly" letters yet). Signed, Helen
- The next time I see someone litter, I will pick up the object dropped and present it to the litterer, saying "Excuse me… you dropped this." Signed, Betty … I will support Betty by having someone else purposely litter in front of her sometime. I will then check back with Betty about what she did. Signed, Dick

This action research/action sequence is significant because it allows you to be divergent in seeking alternative ways of responding to injustice, oppression, and other challenges… and to be convergent in choosing behaviors that make sense for you personally. It also provides a structure in which you can act on what you value.

❑ Activity #125: It's Your Choice

If you want some food for thought regarding social values issues, then chew on the following questions (by yourself and/or in a group)—be sure to take note of the values underlying your choices:

- Would you rather live in a commune or in a condominium?
- If your neighbor dumped trash in your yard, would you pick it up or tell him to pick it up?

- Would you rather smoke or have a car with a bad exhaust system?
- Would you live near a nuclear power plant, if it significantly decreased your electricity bill?
- Would you rather give up 50 percent of your salary to charity or spend a year volunteering through AmeriCorps Service Jobs?
- Would you rather live in a big house, with a little land, or in a small house, with a lot of land?
- Would you rather be wealthy and lonely or poor and have many friends?
- If you were a parent, would you rather have your children be totally honest with you or not give you all the details?
- Would you rather have your children have a good job or a good marriage?
- If you had just been picked up hitchhiking after a long wait and the driver started telling sexist jokes, would you get out of the car or stay in?
- If you saw someone steal something, would you ignore it or confront the thief?
- If you saw a child shoot a bird with a BB gun, would you praise the child, chastise the child, or ignore the situation?
- If you heard one of the staff members put down another, would you stand up for that person, leave the room, or join in?
- In dealing with social issues, do you see yourself more like a rock or leaves in the wind?
- When you die, would you rather have a traditional funeral, be cremated, and/or donate your body to science?
- When you become old, which do you think you will fear the most: poverty, death, loneliness, lingering illness, or being a burden to your children?
- Would you have a mildly disabled parent live with you at home or put her in a nursing home?
- Would you impose your own lifestyle on your children for as long as possible or allow the children free choice from the beginning?
- Would you go out of your way to share your Thanksgiving dinner with people in need or take care of just your own family's dinner?
- Would you sell 40 acres for profit as a subdivision for tract housing or would you sell it at less profit as a wildlife refuge?
- What would be the worst thing you could find out about your teenage son: he wants to work in a weapons factory, he's a persistent litterer, he's an avowed racist, or he pushes hard drugs?
- Respond to the same question for your daughter.
- Would you rather install and maintain a car pollution device or pay more for gasoline?
- Are you more of a spender or saver (of time, resources, energy, money, etc.?
- Would you rather vote for a needed sewage treatment plant or maintain low property taxes?

❑ Activity #126: What Do You Wanna Be When You Grow Up?

Young people are not the only ones who ask this question. There are many adults who are wrestling with tough issues related to work and leisure. The following "favorites grid" may help you, staff, and participants to sort through these issues. Divide a large sheet of construction paper into four squares, and then respond to the questions for each block:

- When you were young, did you have a favorite place, a place you could call your own, perhaps a secret hiding place? What was it that made this place your favorite? Do you have a favorite place now? What makes it special? How does it compare with your first favorite place?
- Who is your favorite person at work, school, or camp? How long has this person been your favorite? What is it about this person that you enjoy? Can you think of ways to enjoy this person even more? Who else does this person remind you of?
- What is your favorite activity at work, school, or camp? What is your favorite leisure activity? Do the two have anything in common? What skills does each call upon? Does either of them involve your favorite person or place?
- When is your favorite time during the week? What makes it special? What are you usually doing or looking forward to at that time? Are there any ways you can think of to have this kind of time occur more frequently during your week? What are the names of the people with whom you've shared this favorite time?

This activity seeks to build on your strengths, resources, and interests. Identifying and sharing favorites can have a nourishing effect on our lives, especially if we can develop ways of maximizing the frequency and intensity of those favorites. Asking, "How can you get more of what you want from life?" is a first step in doing what you want to do as you "grow up."

❑ Activity #127: Are You Someone Who …?

Money is a values area that is full of conflict and confusion. This activity will help you determine what that green picture of George Washington means to you. Divide a sheet of paper in half. Further divide the right side of the paper into two columns, A and B. For each of the statements that describes you, place a check in column A. There are no right or wrong answers—just descriptive data about you for your study.

If you are interested, you may also want to discover how other people see you. You can do this by asking someone you know—friend, family member, co-worker, participant in your program—to put checks in column B next to each item that person thinks describes you (you will have folded over column A). You might be in for some interesting feedback and discussions. Are you someone who …

- Would rather change to a job you didn't like if it offered $10,000 a year more than you now make?

- Would change your lifestyle if your income doubled?
- Is more of a saver than a spender?
- Wants something badly now, but can't afford it?
- Would give money to a beggar?
- Gives money to charities?
- Thinks children should have to work for their allowance?
- Has ever shoplifted?
- Gives money to environmental action groups?
- Believes in a lifestyle of voluntary simplicity?
- Will never want much money?
- Will never get as much money as you want?
- Would spend more than five dollars at a carnival?

Of course, as with the other activities, you can adapt "are you someone who ...?" to speak to other areas of values interest. Are you someone who will do this?

❏ Activity #128: Holiday Autobiography

More and more people seem to feel that holidays "happen" to them. Much of the meaning and value underlying holidays has either been lost or clouded. Holidays can be times of celebration of what is important to us, rather than times in which we go through meaningless motions. If we are to take charge of our lives and our holidays, however, we must be clear about what we value. Developing a deeper self-understanding can help you put the value back in your holidays. Start by taking an inventory of some events from your past. Your autobiographical sketch might be formed around the following kinds of questions:

- Recall as many Thanksgivings as you can. Where did you have dinner each Thanksgiving? Did you ever invite anyone outside the family to dinner? Did your family have any rituals on Thanksgiving? If so, what values were reflected in those rituals (or lack of rituals)?
- Recall all of the holiday presents you have given your parents in the past five years. What presents did you receive as a child that stand out in your mind? What was special about those presents? Which presents have you enjoyed giving the most? What was it that was enjoyable about giving those particular presents? If you could choose something from nature to give as a gift to your parents, children, friends, and/or participants in your program, what would you pick? What gift from nature would you like to receive? What does it signify?
- What did you do on your last five birthdays (your own personal holiday)? In what other ways has celebration entered your life?
- Recall all the ceremonies in which you have taken part.
- At five-year intervals (from age five to the present), list your favorite holidays. Analyze what was special about the holiday for you at each age. Underline those items that still retain their special meaning for you. If this special flavor is currently

missing from your holidays, you may want to consider making a self-contract to build this special quality into the holiday.

- What rituals or ceremonies would you like to see in this school or camp/outdoor education program? What are some ways you think "celebration" could be incorporated into this program? If you could imagine an "ideal day" for you in this program, what would it look like? What can you do to make it a reality?

❑ Activity #129: Epitaph

The goal of this activity is not to have us dwell in morbidity, but rather to reinforce the notion that we are each responsible for the quality of our lives. It is based on the assumption that we all have a lot of living left to do. "On the whole, I'd rather be in Philadelphia," an epitaph that is attributed to W. C. Fields, supposedly captures some of the comedic essence and meaning of his life. What would you want engraved on your tombstone? What would be an accurate nutshell summary of your life? What object from nature would you want on your tombstone—what does this metaphor stand for? Whenever something appears in your epitaph that has not appeared yet in your life, it should be noted. This could represent a potential goal toward which you might work.

❑ Activity #130: Where Do You Draw the Line?

It is very appropriate for people to suppose (wonder) and to expose (share) their values. It is sometimes difficult, however, to draw the line between growth-enhancing values, exploration (supposing and exposing), and inculcation/moralizing (imposing and deposing values).

This activity invites you to take note of the strength of different values issues for yourself, which, in turn, can help you to clarify your boundaries with regard to supposing/exposing/imposing/deposing values. Take a sheet of paper and draw four columns with the following headings: I value and act on this; I'm happy that others value and act on this (although I do not act on it); I am willing to tolerate this; and I will actively fight and oppose this. Place each of the following items in the appropriate column:

- Cheating on income tax
- Reporting the cheater to the Internal Revenue Service
- Vice-principal who makes a student kneel in order to check her skirt length
- College student pushes drugs to pay for his tuition
- Joining segregated swim club
- Littering
- Telling racist jokes
- Killing whales for profit
- Company dumping toxic wastes in rivers
- Doctors who support death with dignity
- Developing nuclear plants
- Shoplifting

- Writing letters to the editor
- Voting in national elections
- Having a curfew for teenagers
- Camp director who paddles campers
- Making your own gifts
- Watching television
- Smoking
- Giving money to charity
- Decriminalizing marijuana
- Sending child to an alternative school
- Sending child to camp each summer
- Texting and driving
- Spending hours each day on Facebook
- Recycling paper and glass

One way to springboard off this activity would be to note the criteria you used in placing each item in the appropriate column—how did you know where to draw the line? You may also want to do an alternative search (see Activity #123) for some of the items—e.g., brainstorm ways of opposing racist jokes, brainstorm ideas for gifts that you could make, etc.

Being clear yourself is the first step toward being able to work with others on emotion-full values issues. This activity is designed to help you explore your values "space," and to aid you in giving others space to explore their values.

❑ Activity #131: To Pick or Not to Pick… That Is the Question

Some plants can be picked with no danger of becoming scarce in an area and others cannot. Many believe that good conservation practice involves maintaining a variety of plants in an area. In order to decide whether to pick a plant or not, a number of questions can be considered.

Distribute and discuss the "Picking Questions." The purpose of the questions is to provide some ideas to ponder before picking a plant. If the answer to a question is "yes," the plant may probably be picked for a particular reason. Decide how many "yeses" are needed in order to pick that plant.

Go outdoors to select a plant and ask the questions. Decide whether to pick the plant at the end of the questioning process. (Caution: If there are rare or protected plants in the area, and you do not want to risk them being picked, take your group to them first and go through the questions to illustrate why that plant should not be picked.)

Picking Questions:

- Are there more than 100 other plants or plant parts of the same kind in the area?
- Can you learn something important from picking it that you could not learn by leaving it?
- Can it be made into a useful product that will benefit people in some way?
- Will the plant be as beautiful as it is now after it is picked?
- Will the whole plant be saved from destruction if I pick it?
- Will the plant die soon and decay?
- Is the plant safe for me to pick?
- Is it all right to pick this plant, even if the answers to all of the other questions were "yes?"
- What will you do now? To pick or not to pick, that is the question.

When the group comes together again, the participants' values may be assessed from their responses to the questions and from the discussion that follows.

❑ Activity #132: Making a Difference

What is values exploration all about? Making a difference. Making a difference in the quality of life … making our lives more value-able. In order to do that, we need to move from "I understand" to "I take a stand." This activity suggests a seemingly simple (to understand), but oftentimes very difficult (to do) way of taking a stand: writing a letter to the editor.

Think about an issue of importance to you. Express your thoughts, feelings, and values around this issue in a letter to the editor—of your local newspaper, a camp newspaper, a school district newsletter, or a magazine. You may want to turn the letter into a petition. It could be a values-clarifying experience for the staff and participants in your program to be presented with the option of signing their names to it. You may want to encourage the staff and participants to come up with their own letters as well. As our nation is in its third century, we will need active, thinking, and questioning citizens, if we are to survive and grow. We will need people who have the courage to address important social values issues, who have the courage to take a stand, who have the ability to make a difference.

OUTDOOR ACTIVITIES

The foregoing indoor lessons often use paper-and-pencil activities and group discussion to achieve their objectives. While these approaches are effective, they can be supplemented by valuing reinforcement outdoors. This section presents specific methods to become involved—both mentally with the valuing processes and physically with the manipulation of related materials and objects. We present them as suggestions—as a beginning.

❑ Activity #133: Putting Your Values on the Line

Go outside and find examples of objects or events that fit somewhere along the following lines. Place these on the line, based on your values. Create other value lines that you discover when you look outdoors.

Ugly _____ Beautiful

Annoying _____ Pleasant

Fast _____ Slow

Offensive _____ Attractive

Mean _____ Kind

Bad _____ Good

How did this exercise help you examine your values? How did it feel to "put your values on the line?"

❑ Activity #134: Object Ranking

Select a twig or leaf from each of three trees in the area. Rank the twigs or leaves, according to their usefulness to you. What criteria were used to determine usefulness? Select specific standards of usefulness (such as toolmaking, shelter-making, survival food or drink, game equipment, and animal food). Select and rank the twigs or leaves according to beauty. Try this with plants other than trees.

❑ Activity #135: Nature's Substitutes

Find or make the best natural substitutes for the following items: a cup; a plate; a spoon; a candle; a nail; and a fish hook. Select other useful items and invent substitutes for them. Use some of the items for a day and evaluate their effectiveness and beauty. How much energy and natural resources could be conserved by using these substitutes? Why do you think more people do not use them?

❑ Activity #136: What Is Noise?

Sit quietly for five minutes. On a pleasant-unpleasant sound continuum, place words or other symbols that describe the sounds you hear and their origin. When all the sounds are placed on the continuum line, mark the point at which noise begins for you. Does this point on the line vary with where you are and how you feel at a particular time? Compare your sound continuum with those of others. Would it be difficult to agree on the definition of "noise" in your group?

❑ Activity #137: Looking Around

Rotate your body slowly in a circle, with your eyes directed above you at a 45-degree angle. Record all of the sights that are pleasing to you during a 360-degree rotation. Do the same thing with your eyes straight ahead. Finally, repeat this activity with your eyes directed toward the ground at a 45-degree angle. In which of the three eye positions did you record the most pleasing sights? Were they natural or made by people or a combination of both? Do your perceptions coincide with those of others?

❑ Activity #138: Place—Thoughts and Feelings

This activity is an opportunity for you to note the impact of the environment on you. Divide a sheet of paper into four columns. In column one, write down five words that describe your thoughts and feelings about a place. Move to three other places and do the same thing in the other columns. After being in four different places, examine the sets of five words. What do you notice about the effect of places on your thoughts and feelings? If you wish, share your descriptions with others. What can you learn about others? About yourself?

❑ Activity #139: Feeling Places

Feeling Places provides a chance for you to legitimize and identify your feelings as one data source in dealing with values. Mark off an area about 15 meters square, containing as wide a variety of environments as possible, e.g., forest, field, pond, stream, etc. In a group setting, ask people to go to the spot that makes them feel the most comfortable, least comfortable, most curious, most angry, most excited, etc. Form clusters of people after each movement and take some time to share your experiences about these places.

❑ Activity #140: Dollar Values

This activity provides you with the opportunity to use a fiscal yardstick to measure what you value in the environment. Find objects in the environment and place dollar values on the three most valuable items. Do this privately, and then share your assessments with others. On what objects was there the most agreement? Most disagreement? Did you find that some objects could not be judged in monetary terms? What terms can be used for those items? How can the degree of value be measured or communicated to others?

❑ Activity #141: Eye/I of the Beholder

Evaluate an area by walking over it. Use the viewpoints of different animals (e.g., deer, rabbits, snakes, squirrels, owls, robins, fox, mice, beaver, and bear). Examine food, shelter, water, space, and other aspects. Evaluate the same area from the human viewpoints of a building contractor, farmer, lumberman, hunter, naturalist, artist, and teacher. Does this mental role-playing cause you to view the environment differently?

❑ Activity #142: Litter Line

Find at least five pieces of litter and arrange them in a line on the ground, according to the most offensive to the least offensive. Then, arrange them according to the most biodegradable to the least biodegradable, and, finally, according to those containing the most abundant natural resources to the least abundant. Can you reach consensus with the group on these rankings? What can you determine about the personal values of those who littered?

❑ Activity #143: Mother Nature Speaks

This activity is a chance for you to step into Mother Nature's shoes—an opportunity to develop empathizing skills. In a group setting, have people pair up. Imagine that a dam is to be built, and that the immediate environment will be flooded and covered with water. Each pair selects an object within everyone's view that they would like to save. List as many reasons as possible for saving that object. Have the members of each pair then tell the rest of the group what it is like to be that object. Becoming the voice of the object, defend its right for existence above water. Have someone else role-play the dam builder and have a dialogue.

❑ Activity #144: Cover Up

Survey an area and note the major ground surface cover in each place (e.g., cement, asphalt, grass, leaves, gravel, etc.). After listing the ground-cover types, rank them according to the following criteria: soil erosion prevention; variety of living things; comfort for sleeping; pleasing color(s); moisture-holding capacity; most acid; and most alkaline. How have people affected the ground surface cover? Predict how the surface cover will look through the seasons of the year.

❑ Activity #145: What Is a Weed?

A weed is a plant out of place, which is considered to be undesirable. Survey the area for weeds and state the reason(s) for labeling them weeds. Is it possible for some people to consider a plant a weed and others not?

❑ Activity #146: Changes

Find three changes people have made in the environment. Will these changes still be visible in five years? How have these changes affected the environment? What things will happen because of the changes? How can people improve the changes? Find evidence of natural changes. How do you feel about change in the environment? Find two changes that animals (other than people) have made. Take 10 steps. Can you see more changes made by animals? Will these changes last more than five years? Will these changes affect other animals? How? How permanent are various changes?

❑ Activity #147: Texture Hunting

Texture in the environment can be discovered by touching objects or by placing paper over them and rubbing with a crayon or pencil. Find four different textures. How would you use these textures if you were a furniture maker? A clothes designer? A painter? A sculptor? What is one job you have thought about doing in your life? How could you use these textures in that job?

❑ Activity #148: Sniffing Around

Choose a partner and look around for three natural objects. Tell your partner which ones you chose. Then, ask your partner to count slowly to 10, while you describe how the objects might smell. Do this for each object. Next, pick one object and go to it. Sniff very carefully, noticing how it smells. Then, give two descriptive words about the smell. Next, let your partner select three natural objects and do the same thing. If you wanted to develop a sharper sense of smell, what are some ways you could do it? Do you both agree on "good" and "bad" smells?

❑ Activity #149: Sketching Progress

Locate a natural area, containing as little development as possible. Is such a place hard to find in your area? Sketch the scene carefully on paper. Then, one by one, add the following objects to the scene by sketching right over the natural scene (do not erase, just draw over the natural scene): a road, picnic site, telephone and power lines, a restaurant, fire hydrant, and traffic light. How has the natural scene changed? How do you feel about the changes? Discuss the pros and cons of "progress."

❑ Activity #150: String Force

Cut a 100-inch piece of string. Using the string as an imaginary fence or boundary, mark off an area that you would like to protect from destruction by urbanization.

❑ Activity #151: Mini-Trail

Take a 100-inch piece of string and select a miniature nature trail route that includes as many points of interest as possible. Guide others along your 100-inch nature trail.

❑ Activity #152: Pleasing Shapes

Make sketches of three aesthetically pleasing tree shapes that you can observe. What characteristics do these trees have in common? Can you find pleasing shapes in other objects?

❑ Activity #153: Shelter Models

Using objects found in the area, build a model of a shelter that incorporates one or more of the following: protection from wind, rain, and snow; visual harmony with nature; human comfort, convenience, or warmth; ease of outdoor viewing; energy conservation; and other important design elements.

❑ Activity #154: Eco-Change

Find five plants or plant parts that can be picked without significantly disturbing (changing) the ecology of the area. Arrange them in a row, according to the one that disturbed the ecology the least to the one that disturbed the ecology the most. What other plants or plant parts were not picked, because they would have significantly disturbed the ecology of the area? What implications does this activity have for your daily life?

❑ Activity #155: Historical Landmarks

Landmarks are chosen and set aside because of their importance to the history of the area. Select one historical landmark (natural or human-made) that should be preserved for its historical value. Share this landmark and its historical importance with others.

❑ Activity #156: Values Theme Hike

One way of making hikes more value-able is through the use of theme cards. Each time you (and/or a group) goes on a hike, take one theme card with you. Three-by-five-inch cards can be used to capture such themes as pleasant sounds, beautiful colors, graceful movements, good changes, useful plants, harmony in nature, ecological balance, eye-catching patterns, peaceful places, happiness, etc. As you walk, look for examples of the theme you carry. Another approach to the values themes might be to look for the opposite of each of the aforementioned "positives," e.g., noise, ugly colors, clumsy movements, bad changes. This exercise is a good way to keep your eyes open to what you value.

❑ Activity #157: Partner Scavenger Hunt

This activity is a modification of the old, but still popular, scavenger hunt. This version is conducted in pairs, so that you can interact with a partner—as a way of encouraging cooperation, keeping observant, and engaging in values decision-making. As with the previous activities, feel free to modify the following form for your own setting and group:

Directions:

This scavenger hunt is different, because before you can locate the items on the list, you and your partner should agree on what to select. Please do not pick any living plants, unless there are hundreds more in the immediate area. If you cannot bring back the actual object, make a sketch or describe it with words. Enjoy the hunt, but most important, enjoy each other. Among the items for which you could "hunt" are the following:
- Two stones that fit together like puzzle pieces
- Two leaves that fell last year from the same tree
- A picture drawn on sandpaper by both partners, using only pigments from nature
- A natural object that both agree is the most beautiful in the immediate area
- Something green or brown that both of you can carry back together
- A poem that you coauthor, based on a common experience outdoors
- Find natural objects and use them to create music together.

- A crayon or pencil-rubbing of an interesting texture
- Make some improvement in the environment together and share it with others.
- Select three highlights from the time you spent together.

❑ Activity #158: Litter Locations

Walk to a relatively undisturbed area outdoors and assign groups of participants to various spots. Give each group a quantity of a specific type of trash (e.g., empty soda cans, paper, plastic six-pack rings, bottle caps, etc.) and ask them to distribute the objects as though they were litterbugs. Allow them ample creative license for deciding how to litter the area. Upon completion of the littering in various locations, gather the group together and have the litterbugs lead the group to their location. Ask the entire group to record the answers to the following questions at each location:
- On a scale of 1 (not at all) to 10 (very much), indicate how much this scene bothers you.
- How could this scene harm wildlife?
- About how long would it take for these objects to decompose, and the area appear natural again?
- What are some reasons a person would throw away this type of litter in the woods?
- How could we solve this type of litter problem elsewhere?

After these questions are answered and discussion is ended, the whole group picks up every piece of litter at that location. The trash may be saved for use with other groups. After visiting all litter locations, further analysis of the data may occur to assess the values of the participants with regard to littering.

❑ Activity #159: "Tree-mendous" Trees

Select a tree and give it a name, based upon something that the tree gives to the world (i.e., shade, lumber, fruit, wildlife shelter). (The name should not be the species name.) Using the "Tree Conversation Sheet," ask the participants to hold a conversation with a tree and record the imagined answers on a tagboard name tag. Be sure that they number each answer to correspond with the questions. After finishing, have them tie the identification tag around the tree trunk, showing the tree name and the answers written boldly with a magic marker or crayon.

Tree Conversation Sheet:
- How are you doing today ….. ? (tree name)
- About how long have you been standing there?
- What gifts do you give to the world?
- Are you more useful to the world dead or alive?
- May I cut you down?
- Why or why not?
- What are three words that describe you best?

- When will I see you again?
- What else would you like to say to me?
- May I draw your picture?

After you have recorded the imaginary conversation with a tree, reassemble the group and walk from one tree to the other to share answers to the questions. (If the group is large, sharing may be done in small groups.) This technique is an excellent way to assess your values concerning particular trees.

❑ Activity #160: Animal Place Value

You will have an opportunity to closely examine a place where a certain animal lives. To find that place, throw a coat hanger, bent into a circle, wherever you want. You may aim the toss or throw it randomly. When you have found a place to examine, follow these instructions:

- Choose an animal that might live in that place.
- Can you find any evidence of that animal or the animal itself? (It is not essential to find the animal or evidence of it to do this activity.)
- What conditions within the circle are necessary for the survival of that animal?
- Imagine each of the life-supporting conditions being removed or polluted one-by-one. How would this affect your animal?
- What could you do to each circle place to make it better suited as a home for your animal? Do it if you can.

When you have completed these directions, share your answers within small groups of three to five participants.

❑ Activity #161: Beauty Seekers

Beauty exists everywhere in common objects, if we take the time to find it. Select an object, such as a plant, rock, area of soil, or piece of wood, and carefully examine it for 10 minutes. An excellent method for examining detail is to sit comfortably with the selected object in view. Then, draw every detail observed with a pencil, *without looking at the paper*. Do not take your eyes from the object throughout the drawing process, even if you pause. It does not matter what the drawing looks like, because this is an exercise in observing detail, as opposed to producing a replica of that object. (Many people are pleasantly surprised at the beauty of the drawing, too.) After the 10-minute observation period, answer the following questions:

- What is beautiful about your object?
- Is it hard to believe that no other object in the world is exactly like this one?
- Can you do something to your object to make it more beautiful? If so, what?
- Examine your object for one minute more. Can you find more beauty in it?
- Do you believe that "beauty is within the eye of the beholder?" If so, how are you like the object you observed?

❑ Activity #162: Auto-matic Ecology Challenges and Opportunities Panel

We live in an automobile-dominated society. Car emissions play a significant part in producing greenhouse gases, which, in turn, play a significant role in the health of the planet. It would be healthy to invite individual participants to think about this factor and to encourage participants to think-out-loud about this in your group. For the think-out-loud discussions, you could go outside and have one-on-one, walk-and-talk time with different people on different topics.

Since the "different-values-for-different-folks" catchphrase is true, it would be important for any of these panel discussions to be based on the guideline of identifying and cherishing what you have in common, while simultaneously respecting and appreciating differences. Use the following topics to get started:

- How important would it be to you to have a car that gets great gas mileage? Even if it cost $10,000 more than a car that gets fewer miles per gallon?
- Would you consider taking public transportation more often, if it helped reduce your car's carbon footprint?
- Would you consider buying a Tesla or another electric car? Why or why not?
- Do you think it would be a good idea to lower air pollution standards in order to increase mileage?

Examples of other ecology thought-and-discussion starters include the following:

- Do you think recycling is a good idea? Do you currently recycle?
- If you do think that recycling is positive, what recommendations do you have to encourage people to do it more consistently in their lives?
- Do you believe that air pollution standards should be lowered in order to produce needed energy? Should we prioritize the production of coal or renewable energy sources, like solar and wind energy? What are the pros and cons of each?
- Where would you prefer to live—in a large city or in the wilderness? Why?
- What policy do you think your community should have: no-growth or unlimited expansion and development? Please explain your rationale.
- What are three things you can do to improve the health of the planet?

❑ Activity #163: Action-Learning

Action-learning means becoming involved in meaningful group projects that provide opportunities to act upon important values. These projects deal with felt needs and desirable values in the camp or school setting. Once a list of desirable values is made, action-learning projects can be planned cooperatively with participants and staff. Examples of values and related projects include the following:

- Value: Rare and endangered plants and animals should be protected.
- Project: Identify plants to be protected along a nature trail.

- Value: Local plants and animals and their habitats should be studied in ways that lead to knowledge and appreciation.
- Project: Set up mini-habitat terrariums showing some of the local environments to explore.

- Value: People should preserve the natural beauty of the area by doing conservation and beautification work.
- Project: Do a service project to correct an environmental problem.

- Value: Ecological diversity should be maintained or increased, whenever possible.
- Project: Attempt to increase the plant and animal life through plantings and management practices.

- Value: Local streams, lakes, and other water supplies should be protected from contamination by pollutants.
- Project: Monitor the water for pH, temperature, animal life, etc., over a period of time to detect pollution.

- Value: Natural materials should be used to enhance the aesthetic environment.
- Project: Gather natural materials for table centerpieces in the dining hall or cafeteria.

- Value: Collections of natural objects should be limited by abundance and the human populations using the area.
- Project: Make a display of natural objects that can be collected and used in various craft projects.

- Value: Human activities should be restricted to those that have the least long-range ecological impact on the environment.
- Project: Conduct a survey of the area and make recommendations about human uses.

- Value: Energy should be conserved in as many ways as possible.
- Project: Plan and cook a nutritious meal that wastes as little energy in the food web as possible.

Action-learning has been a part of many camps and outdoor education programs for a long time. Camp leaders could examine the projects that are currently done to uncover the underlying values. The list of important values could be expanded, and new projects implemented to address these values.

SO WHAT'S THE SCORE?

Looking to the outdoors is an excellent way for us to gather insights about what is inside us, about what we value. It is crucial—for us personally and for our society—that we link our "inside" world and our "outside" world. We hope that the activities in this chapter give you a taste for some practical how-tos and stimulate you to create your own.

This chapter provided you with over three score ideas for valuing activities that focus on important environmental and social issues. We sincerely hope that you do not limit yourself to the ideas presented in this chapter. It is crucial that you tap your own creativity, as well as the ingenuity of the staff and participants in your program, in stretching the activities presented in this section. If you do, your score will grow, and everyone will come out a winner.

The following suggestions and questions may provide you with ideas for next steps—where do you go from here?

- Rank-order the activities in terms of their usefulness to you. Think about the criteria you are using in this ranking (e.g., the activity speaks to an issue of real person concern, the activity is one that staff and participants could engage in together, the activity could fit easily into our program in an ongoing way, the activity seems to spark a lot of energy and fun, etc.).
- Take each activity, one at a time. Brainstorm ways that you could make it work for you in your setting. How could the activity be modified, rearranged, combined, or extended to better address your needs?
- Which activities will you do just by yourself? Which ones would you like to share with staff, with participants, with staff and participants together, with friends, with family?
- List the objectives for and strengths of each activity. Are there other ways, or new activities that you could generate, to speak to these same objectives and strengths?
- In what ways could you employ nature and your immediate environment in the activities?
- How can you change an activity so that the process will remain the same, but the content of the activity would be different (e.g., using the process of the moral dilemma story with different values issues)?
- What will your first steps be in springboarding off the ideas presented in this chapter? Make a contract with yourself and/or another person (see Activity #124). What is your action plan?

> *"It is important to value what you do and to do what you value."*
>
> —Sid Simon

GIVING CREDIT WHERE CREDIT IS DUE

The authors are indebted to the following pioneers in the values clarification and humanistic education fields: Louis Raths, Sid Simon, Merrill Harmin, Howie Kirschenbaum, and Leland Howe. They inspired us to create and adapt many values clarification exercises for this book. Check the extensive Resources chapter in our companion book (*Humanizing Outdoor and Environmental Education*) for information on many of their books.

For the "Values Sheets" (Activity #122), we appreciate the stimuli that came from Merrill Harmin, Sid Simon, Albert Piltz, Robert Sund, and Glen Dines.

We thank our colleagues who co-authored books and numerous articles with us that have appeared in professional journals and magazines over the decades, including *Learning, Today's Education, Scholastic Voice Teacher's Edition, Today's Catholic Teacher, Adult Leader, The Communicator: Journal of the New York State Outdoor Education Association, Camping Magazine*, etc. Special thanks to Marie Hartwell Walker, Ron Witort, and Bob Hawley.

CHAPTER 6

MAKING FRIENDS WITH YOURSELF: THE NATURE AND NURTURE OF SELF-ESTEEM

"I am larger, better than I thought. I did not know I held so much goodness."

—Walt Whitman

One day, Linus notes that Charlie Brown has been a really dedicated baseball manager, always giving 110 percent to the team. Linus suggests that the team show their appreciation to Charlie by giving him a testimonial dinner. Lucy responds by doubting that he deserves a whole testimonial dinner, and recommends instead that they give him a testimonial snack.

Self-esteem. These two words have become one of the most popular couplings in America today. Everybody likes self-esteem, everybody wants self-esteem. After all, how could you be against it?

In the face of the growing popularity of this dynamic duo, educators, camp leaders, parents, and helping professionals are beginning to explore the nature and nurture of self-esteem. This chapter provides you with at least a testimonial snack, as we look at the what, so what, and now what of self-esteem: what is it? ... so what (so why is it important—why do we need it?)... and now what (now, what are some specific and practical ways to develop it?).

WHAT?

Before plunging into enhancing self-esteem, it makes good common sense for us to first take a look at just what it is we are trying to enhance. The following anecdote illustrates this point:

An airplane pilot delivers this message over the intercom to the passengers on her flight: "Well, folks, we have some good news and some bad news. First, the good: we're making great time! Now the bad news: we're lost."

The first step we need to take is to set up our self-esteem "compass," which will help us find our direction(s). Take a few minutes to fill in the compass that follows—brainstorm all the associations, components, and definitions you have for the concept of "self-esteem"—and place these on the points of the compass.

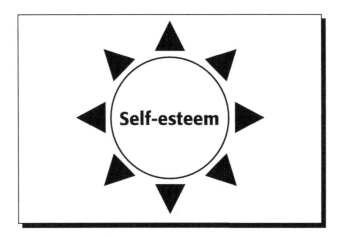

Charlie Brown notes that "In the book of life, the answers are not in the back." There is no "right answer" to the task you just completed—there are probably as many different self-esteem compasses as there are people. It might be an interesting experiment for you to check out your orientation with that of others. For starters, take a look at what we see self-esteem en-compassing:

- *Self-Esteem = Confidence + Competence*: This formula, although it appears to be simple, has important implications. It suggests that if we are to build self-esteem, we must provide opportunities for people to develop confidence (I think I can, I think I can) and competence (I can/do). These two factors are interdependent— the more competent I am, the more confident I feel, which helps me, in turn, to be more competent.

- *Self-Esteem = Successes + Strengths + Dreams:* This formula offers a three-dimensional view of self-esteem. The significant implication is that we must provide chances for people to travel in time, if they are to enhance their self-esteem. Identifying successes from the past can lead to feelings of being success-full (confidence). While growing up, we always heard the phrase "you have to learn from your mistakes." This is important, but it makes just as much, if not more, sense to learn from our successes as well. It is also crucial that we invite people to focus on their present strengths, to build on and maximize their abilities (competence). Finally, we need to support people in setting future goals in actualizing their dreams (confidence + competence).

- *Self-Esteem = Identity + Connectedness + Power:* This compass model also has three directions in which we might move. In helping people to move toward "identity," we seek to offer opportunities for them to develop a sense of worth. If we want people to head toward "connectedness," then we need to provide an environment in which they can feel a sense of belonging. If "personal power" is the goal, then we need to create situations in which people can experience a sense of agency. Of course, it is vital for us to remember that identity, connectedness, and power are interdependent.

SO WHAT?

So what? What's the big deal? Why is it so important that we spend our time and resources in focusing on self-esteem? Haven't we got enough to do already without worrying about this? Are there any compelling reasons for us to commit ourselves to this goal? Yes, there are many.

- *De-valuation:* What we are talking about in this instance is not monetary devaluation, although that may be a concern to many people. Rather, we are talking about the de-valuation of people. Anyone who works with young people (or adults, for that matter) cannot deny the epidemic of people not feeling valuable. This dis-ease manifests itself in a number of ways. Herbert Otto has found that young people can name seven times as many things that are wrong with themselves as things that are right. On another level, suicides, drug abuse, vandalism, child abuse, bullying, cyberbullying, dropping out of school, and increasing violence are manifestations of devaluation. They are symptomatic of people who have given up, who have given up on themselves, who do not value themselves.
- *Killer phrases:* How did this de-valuation come about? What causes it? Unlike the mysterious "Legionnaire's disease," we can quickly identify several culprits. The first one that comes to mind is the seemingly omnipresent "killer phrase." The killer phrase (it could also be a nonverbal look or gesture) serves to put-down another person, to kill a part of that person and her energy or ideas. Oftentimes, killer phrases are given unconsciously or unintentionally. Regardless of the motivation, killer phrases hurt.

What is ironic about killer phrases—and what makes it so hard to confront them—is that they seem to be imbedded in and legitimized by our culture. You needed only to turn on the TV during the 2016 Presidential campaign to get a large dose of the "art" of one-downsmanship. As you probably know, young people (and adults) are quick to pick up on this one-downsmanship mentality.

We recently asked a group of 30 junior high school students to generate a list of killer phrases that are a regular part of their vocabulary. Would you believe they came up with 200 different ones in a three-minute period?! They are constantly bombarded with "you're weird," "you turkey," "what an idiot." Is it any wonder that many people have been brainwashed to believe that they are not worthwhile?

- *Kookie monster:* Perhaps the most insidious effect of the killer phrase is that it creates kookie monsters. This is not the *Sesame Street* variety. Rather, it is the intrapersonal killer phrases with which we hit ourselves. Each of us probably has a little voice (or a big one) within us that at times says: "you're kookie," "you can't do it," "you're dumb," etc. What is insidious about the kookie monster is that we begin to believe it. Furthermore, research has demonstrated the extremely powerful effect of self-fulfilling prophecies. It is crucial that we find ways to help people muffle their kookie monsters and to create positive self-fulfilling prophecies. Or, as Jack Canfield says, to help people become "inverse paranoids"—people who think that the world is out to do them good.

- *Achievement:* There has been a great hue and cry over the years about falling achievement test scores. Teachers and parents have been lamenting openly that "students aren't like they used to be" and that "students just don't have the basic skills anymore." As a result, many schools have picked up the "back-to-basics" banner.

This attitude is an understandable, yet sad and ironic, phenomenon … sad and ironic because we could effectively get "back to basics" by going "forward to fundamentals." In this case, the fundamentals are focusing on those beliefs and feelings that are closest to each one of us—our self-esteem. For, as Canfield notes, they "actually determine who you are! They also determine what you think you are, what you do, and what you can become!" Extensive research indicates that a very strong relationship exists among self-esteem and academic achievements, task performance, and school success.

NOW WHAT?

If one or more of the aforementioned "so what" reasons hits home for you, then you are probably reading these words. Given the nature of and need for self-esteem, what are some practical ways that teachers, camp leaders, helping professionals, parents, and young people can nurture their own and others' self-esteem? We believe that the road to developing self-esteem involves joining the A.A.A. You'll be on the right track if you:

- Have **A**ttitudes conducive to this goal
- Create an **A**tmosphere that encourages the development of self-esteem
- Provide **A**ctivities that encompass the elements of self-esteem described in the "What?" section

❑ Attitudes

The foundation of self-enhancing atmosphere and activities lies in the establishment of self-enhancing attitudes. These attitudes are the most important ingredients in nurturing self-esteem. We encourage you to change the amount of each ingredient when working with different people in different situations. In other words, feel free to tap your own flexibility and creativity in developing your own attitudinal recipes. The following are some ingredients to consider:

- *I know you can, I know you can:* Believing in people and in their potential is crucial. Having confidence in their competence will often build both their confidence and their competence. This attitude can be the primary motivator to help others move from feelings of "I can't do it" to "I can (and will) do it." This attitude implies that you will stick with the person as she takes on new challenges and growth experiences.
- *The message is the massage:* There is so much negativism in the world today, in the form of killer phrases, kookie monsters, and the news on TV, which starts off with a barrage of crimes and distressing events. It has gotten to the point where many people are "numb" to feelings or seeing anything positive about themselves, others, or the world around them.

It is vital that we break through the wall of negativism by having a positive attitude and communicating it in a genuine (not saccharine) way. Hopefully, the positive message will massage the positivity that lies numb or dormant in others. It could be as simple as telling a student or camper what you appreciate about her. Or, it could be mailing or emailing a note to the parents, informing them of their child's achievements—sending them an efficiency report (or opposed to a deficiency report). Or, it could be asking another person to focus on the positive—by asking, "What is new and good in your life?" It just makes good, common sense that positive, nourishing seeds—rather than toxic ones—are at the root of helping humans to grow, to learn, and to love.

- *1 + 1 is better than 1 - 1:* At first glance, most people would agree that it is better to build and to be synergistic, rather than to tear down and to be destructive. At times, however, there is a difference between what we would like to do and what we are likely to do. Enter the culprit: Yes, but …

  "Yes, *John has made a good point there,* but *it's not in the budget."*

  "Yes, *that's a nice idea, Betty,* but *we've already tried it."*

  "Yeah, *I could go along with you on that,* except *that no one else will like it."*

  How different it would be if we were no longer the but (sic) of killer phrases. Wouldn't it be nice if we had "but" butt out of our vocabulary? One might now say, "*Yes, but* what would replace it?" The word "and" could be a simple addition to our vocabulary to accomplish this purpose. Note the change in tone between the following statements and those aforementioned:

  "Yes, *John has made a good point there,* and *we need to explore ways of financing it."*

  "Yes, *that's a nice idea Betty,* and *let's take some time to generate new wrinkles, based on our past experience with it."*

  "Yeah," *I could go along with you on that,* and *we ought to figure out how to enlist others' support."*

  "Yes, and …" statements put the accent on the positive and on constructive problem-solving. They add energy to a situation and to people. They motivate people to work together, to give support to one another, and to develop their own creativity.

- *Beware of the Scylla and Charybdis of self-esteem:* In using our compass to chart our self-esteem course, it is vital that we be aware of two cultural obstacles: perfectionism and modesty.

  Although many of us have heard the phrase, "No one is perfect," there is sometimes a tendency to attach a rider: "No one is perfect (but I should be)." Perfectionists are made, not born … a child brings home a paper with a "98" on it, and the parent asks, "What happened to the other two points?" … a young person playing in a Little League game makes some good fielding plays, but the coach only remarks on the one error. Perfectionism leads people to drop out ("if you don't try, then you can't fail"), to procrastinate (in order to postpone coming to grips with one's imperfection), and to fall into the "winning is everything" syndrome (which makes people forget that "it's how you play the game" that is important). What we need to do is to combat the perfectionism syndrome by helping people develop the "courage to be imperfect."

At the same time, we need to be aware of a cultural norm that appears almost as an 11th commandment: "Thou shalt not brag, because thou might become conceited, stuck up, and a snob." Unfortunately, many people have carried this to an extreme, to a point where they are totally unable to recognize *any* of their strengths and good qualities. The modesty norm leads people to self-depreciating patterns (complete with kookie monster tapes) and interpersonal relationships, based on one-downsmanship (complete with killer phrases). The need is to help people acknowledge, accept, and build on their strengths and to learn from their successes. Ultimately, this approach would lead people to believe and live by the following quotation: "You don't have to blow out my candle to make yours grow brighter."

❏ Atmosphere (Interpersonal Climate)

We have confidence that you can identify many ingredients of a "nurturing atmosphere." Take some time to do a memory scan of a part of your own life. What are some occasions, times, places, or experiences in which you have flourished, grown, reached toward your potential? What was it like then? What in the environment/atmosphere contributed to your growth and self-esteem? Jot down some of the characteristics of the environment that you found nourishing.

In drawing on our own experience, we have also created a picture of a self-enhancing atmosphere. We invite you to expand your own picture by considering the following necessary, but not sufficient factors, which are ways of operationalizing the four attitudes presented in the previous section:

- Success-full: Opportunities to succeed, to engage in risk taking, and to set important goals in taking on challenges are important elements in building feelings of success. If we maximize the chance of success for each individual, then we will have more "success stories."
- Respect: An environment that is full of wonder and that appreciates the dignity of the individual is a vital environment—and is vital to enhancing self-esteem.
- Comfort and caring: Caring, mutual support, empathic listening, and genuineness are at the heart of enhancing self-esteem. If a person feels safe (physically and psychologically), if a person feels comfortable (able to comfort others and to be comforted), if a person trusts (self and others), then that person will be more likely to take risks and to support others, as they take risks in growing.
- Democracy: It is important that democracy not be a "spectator sport" in our schools, camps, and homes. For us, democracy connotes shared decision-making, having a sense of control over your own destiny, cooperation, pluralism, and equity. It seems

clear that if people have chances to make choices freely, to make collaborative decisions, and to have some control over their destiny that they, in turn, will develop a greater sense of worth, belonging, and agency.

- Unconditional positive regard: We need to create an atmosphere in which people are appreciated for who they are, not what they ought to be. This has important implications for those of us who work with young people—we need to care by taking care not to impose our needs, values, and "shoulds" or "ought to's" on them.

- Touching experiences: It makes sense to us to use common sense, that is, the common sense of touch to help people reach out to one another. We need to move gently, yet firmly, in this area—inviting people to literally and figuratively "get in touch" with one another. It could be as simple as a teacher making it a point to shake the hand of each student as she arrives in the morning, or the camp counselor placing a hand on the shoulder of a camper who is having difficulty.

- Making lemonade: One of our favorite quotes is "If life hands you a lemon, squeeze it, and make lemonade." What this means is that we need to avoid dwelling on mistakes, on the negative—and move on to focusing and acting on the positive.

- Different strokes: Different people learn in different ways. Self-esteem is learned. Therefore, different people learn self-esteem in different ways. One implication of this inference is that the self-enhancing environment could be a "variety show," in which the pacing and spacing are varied, and in which people have opportunities to work and learn in different arenas (e.g., individual work, small-group work, large-group work).

- You + more: We find it helpful to take ourselves with a grain of salt. Humor frees our attention and frees us to appreciate ourselves more. Nourishing humor can be an excellent vehicle to help you feel more self-esteem, energy, creativity, and connectedness with others. We aim to create an atmosphere that is light and lively, informal and filled with laughter.

- Encouragement: Encouragement is any action or statement that shows respect, trust, and faith in the person and her abilities, worth, and dignity as a human being. Encouragement emphasizes the process of learning at least as much as the product. Encouragement focuses on what a person can do, rather than what she cannot do, i.e., the glass of water is three-fourths full, rather than one-fourth empty. We look for the donut, not the hole.

We encourage you to play around with these ten guidelines—in doing so, you will be playing with a full deck in creating nourishing environments.

ACTIVITIES

Each activity presented in this section is a way of putting into practice the attitudes and atmosphere described in the previous sections. They will help you to head in one (or more) of the directions on our self-esteem compasses:

❑ Activity #164: The Magic Lamp

The magic lamp is a pantomime activity, in which the participants act out one of their favorite activities or the thing they are good at doing. An imaginary genie's lamp is rubbed as each person, in turn, acts out something. When people in the group think they know what the favorite activity or thing the person is good at doing is, they join in silently and act out the same activity, but extend the movements so that the originator of the idea knows that the activity has been guessed.

For some participants, this game presents problems, because either they can't think of their favorite activity, or they, on occasion, can't think of something they are good at doing. If this situation occurs, others in the group can whisper suggestions to the person. The game could become more complex, if the participants act out something that individual staff members do well and then ask the group to guess to whom that action belongs. Further modifications of the game include acting out favorite animals, program activities, or any other category selected.

❑ Activity #165: Plaque, Not Flak

We have observed that people usually receive far more flak than plaques, even though the plaques are richly deserved. This exercise involves a "field trip." Venture outside and try to find something in the world of nature that would serve as a "plaque to yourself"—something that you could put up in your office, home, classroom, or camp cabin to remind you that you are lovable and capable. Be sure to check the IALAC (I Am Lovable And Capable) story in Chapter 1 of our companion book, *Humanizing Outdoor and Environmental Education*. A variation of this would be for you to search for an appropriate "plaque" for someone else—a friend, a family member, a cabin-mate, a teacher, etc. This approach might even develop into a "good habit"—exchanging plaques with one another, rather than flak.

❑ Activity #166: Food for Thought

This exercise consists of two parts: a provocative stimulus (e.g., a quote from a book or newspaper, a movie, a song, a picture, etc.), followed by a series of thought-provoking questions (which all have a form of the word "you" in them, and are non-moralizing—there is no one "right answer" to the questions). We offer you a sample "Food-for-Thought" sheet that focuses on self-esteem. We hope it whets your appetite so that you will create your own. You can process "Food-for-Thought" sheets, either individually (e.g., place them in a personal journal) and/or with others (their ideas might give you additional food for thought).

> *The human being is made up of oxygen, nitrogen, phosphorus, hydrogen, carbon, and calcium. There are also twelve and one half gallons of water, enough iron to make a small nail, about a saltshaker full of salt, and enough sugar to make one small cube. If one were to put all of this together and try to sell it, the whole thing would be about one dollar.*

- Do you believe that you are worth more than one dollar? Explain.
- When do you feel most worthwhile? With whom do you feel most worthwhile?
- Can you think of some ways to help others feel more worthwhile?
- Some people feel that they are not worth even a dollar. Do you have any ideas about how you might respond and support them?
- If you were to create an advertisement that proclaimed your resources and strengths, what would it say?

❑ Activity #167: Self-Metaphors and Similes

Metaphors are powerful tools, which we can use to enjoy new and creative perspectives on ourselves and our world. This exercise seeks to help you reinforce feelings of "I like me" by asking you to complete an "I am like a _____ because _____" statement. In essence, you have a chance to write a positive metaphor: what do you *like* about yourself, and what from the world of nature is *like* you? We have listed some responses from adults and young people who have done this—to give you some of the delightful flavor of this exercise.

> *I am like the edelweiss that grows high upon the mountain. People have to dare and risk hazardous trails to reach me. I grow above the tree line, in the soft spots between the rocks, in the cold air of eternal winter. But, my petals, though strong as leather, are as soft as velvet for those who reach me.*

> *I'm a leaf. Time brings about change. Sometimes, I'm a leaf among many leaves. Life is full. The trees are in bloom. So am I. A part of it all. Fall is inevitable. At times, I fall from the tree. Parting. Leaving. Winter and I'm gone. The time when I still exist. Somewhere. But not where I can be easily seen. Spring comes. With warmth. And sun. And joy. And I grow and come out again.*

> *I am a stream—I have a surface that everyone can see. But, there are many things going on underneath that surface. I am one stream—within that stream are many different currents that flow at different speeds and in different directions. I hope to get in touch with my own flow.*

> *I am like the wind. I can be as noticeable as a hurricane or as unassuming as a light breeze. I can go anywhere. It's my choice. People are concerned about me and like to hear the daily forecast, yet I'm unpredictable and like myself that way.*

> *I am like a storm in the sense that I will work fast and furious for a given length of time on a certain task—and then die out and do almost nothing for a while. During periods of activity, I begin slowly, work gradually up to a fever pitch, push the project to completion, and then disappear from it altogether.*

I am like a skateboard. My colors are sometimes bright and fascinating. Other times, I am colored in subdued hues. My wheels take me to many places at so many different speeds—weaving, turning, spinning. Sometimes, I just like to move quietly and slowly, my wheels hardly turning. I love to take people for a ride, even though they knock me over sometimes.

I am a volcano—sometimes, I lie dormant, other times, I erupt. I can get angry and erupt with red hot lava. Even when I am dormant, a lot of bubbling and turmoil is going on inside me. I am somewhat predictable, and, most of the time, I am stable, just standing there. I try to take things, in rather than erupt, but, sometimes, I can't take any more and have to shout back. I am part of the earth, which is always changing.

❏ Activity #168: Meeting of the Metaphors

The word "validation" is an important one for us. Validation involves accepting and appreciating yourself and others. If you don't receive enough validation, then you run the risk of becoming an self-esteem in-valid. Self-metaphors provide a vehicle for us to validate ourselves. We can springboard off that exercise, and call a meeting of the metaphors, if we want to practice validating others.

The way it works is: you get together with others who have written self-metaphors. Everybody puts their self-metaphors in a pile. The metaphors are "shuffled," and then each person picks one. Now take some time to write a response, a validating response to this person's self-metaphor. Your validation should reflect empathic listening/reading on your part. Try to express ways that you support, identify with, and/or appreciate this other person. Respond as if you are talking directly to the metaphor itself. When everyone has finished, put the papers back in the pile. People can then fish out their original metaphor.

Variations of this exercise include: having more than one person respond to each self-metaphor and having people read the self-metaphors and responses aloud to the whole group (some people are willing to take a bit more risk by guessing who wrote the metaphor and the response). We encourage you to evolve your own variations. In any case, the intent of this exercise is to help people to feel listened-to and validated, to help people build their validation muscles, and to provide a chance for people to be response-able. The following are the responses that were given to the aforementioned self-metaphors:

• *Dear Edelweiss,*

You sound worth reaching. You seem to have a nice combination of strength, support, and beauty. As a caterpillar, methinks I would enjoy hiking (or when I'm older, flying) up to meet you.

Happy Fall, Caterpillar

- *Dear Leaf,*

  I sense a combination of moods in your poem. A concern with change from happy to sad, from sad to happy. I'm glad that after "falling off" and hibernating, you "come out again." I too am like a leaf. I think many of us are. Let's create our own spring.

  In spirit, The Stream

  P.S. If you need a ride, you can float on me.

- *Dear Stream,*

  It must be exciting to be a stream, to have the different speeds and directions from which to pick. To choose what fills your needs, when you are needing. Getting in touch with your flow probably will make you more aware of what choices you have …

  Smooth flowing! The Cocoon

- *Dear Wind,*

  I enjoy the feeling your description of yourself imparts to me. I can feel your looseness and freedom and the good feeling about yourself. You seem spontaneous and open and happy, and have a clear understanding of yourself and your relation to others. I like you, too.

  Love, The Shoe

- *Dear Storm,*

  I admire your task-orientation. Further, I can sympathize with your dormant periods. One who works at a fever pitch must also at times rest and replenish his stores of energy.

  Sincerely, The Bee

- *Dear Skateboard,*

  I admire your variety. It must be fun to be like the rainbow. Having the opportunity to be a variety of colors is so exciting. Traveling and seeing so many things is so adventurous. How much knowledge and fun you must have gained. You're lucky that you experience so many feelings. Weaving, turning, spinning, and then, for the more passive end of it, going quietly and slowly. I'm glad, too, that you can handle people's indifference, as well as their respect.

  Have fun! The Fire

- *Dear Volcano,*

  I, too, have sometimes felt blocked and then must explode or die. Volcanoes can be a creative force—the islands of the Pacific are all formed by volcanoes, and think of Mt. Fuji—that volcano must have inspired thousands of paintings and poems. Can this frustration bubbling within you be used to motivate you to control some of the forces angering you? Can you decide to communicate your distress when you feel it—not be afraid to reveal this inner you? Then, maybe your potential will flow more freely like lava.

  With love, Afghan

❏ Activity #169: Validation Tag

Validation Tag is another exercise to limber up your validation muscles in a group setting. The object of this game is for everyone to get tagged—that is, to get tagged with a validation. One person starts off as the "tagger" (we try to avoid using the word "it," since "it" is such a de-personalizing word). The "taggers" start to run—in slow motion. When the tagger hooks up with a tagee, everyone freezes and listens to the tagger's validation of the tagee. The tagee then assumes the tagger's role and looks for another person to tag with a validation. The game ends when each person has had a chance to be a tagger and tagee.

❏ Activity #170: Gift-Giving

This activity is a good way to build on "I'm okay, you're okay" feelings. Divide a sheet of paper into 10 columns. In the first column, list 10 persons who are very close to you—people who touch your life frequently and/or intimately. In the second column, note the last gift you have given each person—if you have not given a person a gift, then write "none." In the third column, make note of a "gift" you think each person on your list has (e.g., the ability to do carpentry work, a wonderful sense of humor, easy-going, etc.). In the fourth column, note what nature-related metaphor would symbolize the "gift" that is listed in column three (e.g., carpentry work—a beaver; sense of humor—a monkey; easy-going—a leaf fluttering in the air). In the fifth column, list a "gift" that you would like to give each person (e.g., being able to listen better, learning to laugh more easily, being able to "flow" with what's happening). The sixth column gives you a chance to choose a natural metaphor that would represent the "gift" in the previous column (e.g., listen better—rabbit ears; laugh more easily—a hyena; being able to flow—a stream). In the seventh column, write the gift that each person on your list might see in you (this is the flip side of the third column). In the eighth column, put the metaphors that would capture the essence of each of these gifts listed in the preceding column. In the ninth column, indicate if you had to make a guess, what do you think each person would wish you had more of in your life? Finally, in the tenth column, specify what metaphorical gift they could offer you that would communicate the wishes in the ninth column.

This exercise helps you to generate a great deal of data about what gifts you have (strengths and successes), what gifts you would like to receive (dreams and goals), what gifts others have (validating them), and what gifts you might want to give. In looking at the mass of data, what clues emerge as to how to make gift-giving more meaningful in your life? What are your initial steps?

How much joy can come from giving a gift that is valuable to the receiver, and from receiving a gift that you value? Indeed, the joy can be in both the giving and receiving. We present this 10-column grid as a gift to you—to deck the halls of your own life.

❑ Activity #171: Inquiring Reporter

Siphotography/iStock/Thinkstock

Questions are powerful tools. We can use them to "get to the bottom of things"—to dig beneath the avalanche of killer phrases in order to uncover our strengths and successes.

Take some time—either by yourself or with others—to brainstorm as many questions as you can think of that would invite people to discover their "positive side." When you have finished, sort through your list and pick out four favorite questions for evoking a positive response. These could be the ones that would help a person to see herself in a new positive light, ones that would highlight her significant strengths and successes, or ones that seem to capture several strengths at once.

Next, consider what can you do with these questions? That's a good question. The following are some options:

- Why not conduct a self-interview? Ask yourself the very questions that you have generated. Who knows—this might even turn into an ongoing self-validating habit in your life.

- In a group setting (e.g., classroom, cabin meeting, family room, staff meeting, etc.), take time to interview as many people as you can—using the questions you have chosen. This task could be accomplished either by having people informally milling around or by having a more structured environment (e.g., in pairs, each person serves as the interviewer for five minutes, and then is interviewed for five minutes—after which, everyone would change partners).
- It might be interesting to conduct some person-on-the-street interviews—either with people you know well and/or with acquaintances.

For example, you might be interested in a couple of nine-year-olds who used this positive-thinking reporter idea in a neighborhood newspaper that they published for over 200 subscribers. Here are a few of the questions they asked to help people focus on the positive side of their lives—and the responses from their peers:

- Q. What is your favorite hobby? Why?
  A. Making models, like boats and airplanes. I think it's interesting and it requires skill. It's something to be proud of when you're through.
  A. Carving is my hobby, because I like to create things.
  A. Archery—it's fun, it helps me physically and mentally.
  A. Art is my favorite, because I like to use my fingers.
  A. Collecting fossils and shells. They're interesting to study.
  A. Horseback riding—because I like horses.
- Q. Where would you like to go on your ideal vacation? Why?
  A. I would like to go to Florida, because my grandmother lives there.
  A. Washington, D.C.—my best friends are there.
  A. Camp—because I want to go waterskiing.
  A. Somewhere in Europe, because I've never been there before and I think it would be interesting.
  A. Spain—I've learned the Spanish language, and I think it's very interesting.
  A. Disneyland—because I've read a lot about it, and it's exciting.

Although these questions are seemingly simple, they are not simplistic. They invite people to focus on their strengths, interests, and goals. A group of teenagers with whom we worked generated the following additional questions:

- What do you like to do?
- What are your favorite possessions?
- What do you value more than anything else?
- What kind of lifestyle do you think you will follow?
- What is your philosophy of life?
- If you only had three minutes to give your autobiography, what would you say?
- What type of personal ideals do you hold?
- Who do you most admire?

- What makes you laugh?
- What beautiful thing have you done for someone?
- What makes you happy?
- Who is one person you care for?
- What do you want to be when you grow up?
- What's your favorite part of being with people?
- When and where have you been the happiest?
- What do you like about yourself?
- What was the highlight of the last week for you?
- What dreams do you have?
- What helps to bring you up?
- Have you been doing anything interesting or fun?
- What metaphor would describe how you see yourself in the past few weeks?
- What is unique about you?
- If you could watch a movie of yourself in the last two weeks, what would you like about it? What would you change?
- What's been the most consequential, long-reaching thing you've done lately?
- Where would you like to live?
- What are 10 things you most like to do?
- Who do you love?
- Who loves you?
- What do you do for recreation and relaxation?
- What do you look for in a good friend?

The role of inquiring reporter is crucial in this exercise. The interviews will maximize positive sharing and growth if the reporter exhibits the following attributes: listens emphatically and empathically—honestly and warmly; gives the respondent space—by this, we mean that the person being interviewed has a right to respond and a right *not* to respond (to pass on any question); and encourages the respondent to focus on the positive, Killer phrases and kookie monster are out of bounds in this exercise.

We have used the positive questions generated by students and campers as the heart of numerous curriculum units and lessons. Again, it is such a simple—but revolutionary— idea that young people will have more energy, motivation, and commitment to working on questions that come out of and that affect their own lives. That is the power of a good question. It has a way of hooking people's interest.

❏ Activity #172: You Asked for It

In this activity, what you are going to get is an interview, if you ask for it. We know of many teachers, camp leaders, and parents who springboard off the inquiring reporter exercise by establishing the positive interview as a recyclable ritual.

For instance, Mary Ann Baker, a second grade teacher in Edgemont, New York, schedules interviews on a regular basis. Students volunteer to be interviewed by their peers by signing up on a schedule. The interviewee assumes a focal position in the room, and then responds to (or passes on) the questions from her classmates. When the interviewee chooses to end the session, she simply says, "Thank you for your questions." The questions are all aimed at values and value—helping the interviewee to clarify what she values and supporting the interviewee in seeing her own value.

We have also worked with groups of adults, as well as groups of adults and young people together, in which interviewing takes place in pairs or in a quartet (in addition to the large-group format). Following the interview, we find a review to be a nice way of reaching closure—a review of what the interviewer likes/appreciates about the interviewee and what she said. When done in a large group, this kind of "strength bombardment" can be very reinforcing.

The following potential interview questions were generated by a group of adults in a graduate course that Joel taught at Bowling Green State University. We invite you to use these—or better yet, to create your own. We hope these questions whet your appetite for making the family dinner table, the classroom, the camp cabin, or the office more nourishing places to be:

- When are you happiest in your job?
- What makes you feel successful?
- What would make you happier?
- What is important in the innersphere of your life?
- What inspires you? When was the last time you were inspired?
- Why did you decide to go into your work?
- What do you do for leisure? What do you enjoy about that?
- What do you feel you are doing to better this world?
- What do you want to do with your life?
- Who are some people who have positively influenced you?
- If you could change your age, what age would you be?
- What is the one thing you like about yourself?
- What would you do if you won the lottery?
- What is one wish that you have?
- What do you see yourself doing five years from now?
- Are there some things that you do now that you would like to change?
- When you are home and no one else is there, what do you really like to do?
- What kinds of vacations do you like?
- What are the good qualities of your job (or school or camp) that make you enthusiastic?
- What do you like to do for fun?

- If you could do only one thing today, what would you do?
- Who/what was the guiding force in shaping your ideas about raising children?
- If you had one day to live, what would be the first thing you would want to accomplish?
- Who do you admire? What values do they have that you think are important?
- What is the best time of day for you? Why?
- Who are you?
- What do you feel is the most important part of parenting?
- How would you personally define success?
- What has been the most important event in your life?
- What quality in yourself would you like to see in others?

Positive interviews can lead to positive intraviews—everyone can have the feeling of being on "meet the prez." If you elect to "meet the press" in your family, school, camp, or job, then you may very well become the "prez-elect." Do you want to have a self-esteem inauguration? Give yourself a vote of confidence today.

❏ Activity #173: Can and Able

This strategy is an opportunity for you to gain confidence in your competence. Divide a sheet of paper in half. On the left, make a list of all the things you can do. Brainstorm—and post a "no trespassing" sign for the kookie monster. Next, fold the sheet over, so that only the right side shows. Give the paper to another person, and ask her to make a list of all of your abilities of which they are aware. At the same time, you could generate a list of -able words for your partner (e.g., loveable, enjoyable, music-able, sports-able, etc.).

It might prove interesting for you to compare your list of "can" and "able" words. What do the lists tell you about yourself? Are there any strengths that were hidden from you that your partner was able to see? Sometimes, it helps to have another person to point out or confirm our strengths—confirmation can lead to self-affirmation.

❏ Activity #174: Collage Degree

One way to legitimize your incredible competence is to give yourself a credible collage degree. This exercise makes use of the collage, as a creative medium, for patting you on the back. The only treble (sic) with collages is that some people are tired of the ol' magazine cut-and-paste route. So, for this exercise, we will strike a different note—be natural.

Go on a solo hike through your environment. Collect objects from the world of nature that reflect your cans and ables. These objects will serve as the instruments of your collage. Take some time to orchestrate them into a collage. The end product could serve as your collage degree. It might be fun for others to try to guess what competencies your collage symbol-izes. This exercise could even turn into an enjoyable game—a la name that tune—a sharp way to drum up support for yourself and your strengths.

❑ Activity #175: Home Sweet Home

Home Sweet Home is a way for you to explore your own immediate environment—an opportunity to undertake a scavenger hunt for clues as to what enhances your self-esteem. Draw a map of your local environment (it could be of an area as small as your home, or of an area as large as your neighborhood). Do not worry if your map does not look like the official Rand McNally version—just as long as you can understand it.

Take some time to place the following symbols on your map: a "+" next to the spot(s) where you feel nourished, where you feel yourself to be most lovable and capable (if you wish, you could even put sub-symbols—e.g.; a "W" for where you feel a sense of worth; a "B" for where you feel a sense of belonging; and an "A" for where you feel a sense of agency). Next, put a "T" for where you spend most of your time; an "E" to mark the spot(s) that you would like to explore in more depth; a "G" for those areas in which you give a lot of yourself, in which you give/support/nourish others; an "M" in the places where you would like to see more nourishment for yourself; an "H" on the spot where you experienced a high point in the past week; and an "X" on those places that are toxic to you.

The following are some questions to guide your study of the map and aforementioned symbols. We hope that they will aid you in tracking down ways of enhancing your self-esteem:

- In looking at the symbols you have placed, do any patterns emerge? What do the patterns tell you?
- What characterizes the spots where you have placed a "+"?
- Are there ways you can re-arrange your life so that you could spend more time in the "E" places?
- Is there anything you can do to affect the environment in the places where you placed an "M" or an "X"?
- Will you choose to spend less time in the "M" and "X" places?
- Is there anything you can do to make more "high points" occur for you in your life?
- What do you think would happen if you were to place a "G" in the areas where you have marked an "M" or "X" (in other words, if you sought to reach out to others and offer them nourishment)?
- What does "home" mean to you?
- What helps you to feel "at home"—with yourself and others?
- How does your map compare with others who share the same environment with you—do any patterns emerge in looking at each other's maps?
- Are there any goals you want to address as a group?

This exercise seeks to put the cart-ography before the horse. We hope that your map will help you create environments that will enhance self-esteem. We think that this lesson in top-ography will pay off—in helping you to feel "on top of things."

❏ Activity #176: You-Turn

We turn now to an activity that will help you to focus on your dreams and goals. As you look ahead to them, we also encourage you to use your rear-view mirror to learn from and build on the turning points in your life to date. Inevitably, up the road a piece, you will encounter choice points and potential turning points. Learning from your past mistakes, and, more importantly, from your past successes, may give you some clues about which way to turn.

Two roads diverged in a yellow wood,
And sorry I could not travel both
And be one traveler, long I stood
And looked down one as far as I could
To where it bent in the undergrowth;

Then took the other, as just as fair,
And having perhaps the better claim,
Because it was grassy and wanted wear;
Though as for that the passing there
Had worn them really about the same.

And both that morning equally lay
In leaves no step had trodden black;
Oh, I kept the first for another day!
Yet knowing how way leads on to way,
I doubted if I should ever come back.

I shall be telling this with a sigh
Somewhere ages and ages hence:
Two roads diverged in a wood, and I—
I took the one less traveled by,
And that has made all the difference.

—Robert Frost

In a sense, every moment of our lives is a potential turning point. Take some time to think about, write about, and/or discuss the following questions:
- How many major turning points can you identify in your own life?
- What made them turning points—and what "trail markers" do they leave to help you identify future turning points?
- Did you know that they were turning points at that time—or only in hindsight?
- If you had to project, what choice points will you be facing in the future?
- What from your previous experience will help you when you encounter them?
- What might you begin to do next—or continue to do—to prepare for these future turning points?

The point around which this exercise turns is that you have control (and responsibility) over what happens to you. You can be conscious and conscientious in taking charge of you and your life. We urge you to continue to engage in dream of consciousness exercises. Always remember that you can make your own luck. This sense of agency is an important ingredient of self-esteem.

❏ Activity #177: Pollution Alert

Pollution Alert is an invitation for you to establish a tradition, a commitment to patrol and "clean up" the human environment. Your job, if you choose to accept it, Mr./Ms. Phelps, is to identify and weed out killer phrases, kookie monsters, and structures that are toxic to human growth. Your patrol may want to make a regular report to others on examples of human pollution that you have discovered.

For example, you might record the number and kinds of put-down phrases that exist in a particular area (e.g., home, classroom, camp cabin, with friends). Note the effect the killer phrases have on the people who receive them and on the group as a whole. Perhaps, you could even engage in an alternatives search to explore ways of avoiding/minimizing killer phrases.

❏ Activity #178: Moratorium on Bad Breath

This action-project is very simple to understand, but probably very difficult to do. How long can you go without saying a killer phrase? How long can your group avoid uttering put-downs? How long can you go without hearing muttering from your kookie monster? What we are asking you to do is challenge yourself—to see how long you can hold your breath, when it comes to levying killer or kookie monster phrases. This moratorium could be a matter of life and breath.

❏ Activity #179: You're Something to Brag About

One way to combat killer phrases and kookie monster phrases is to add humor to your life—by participating in a tongue-in-cheek bragging practicum—a chance to salute yourself in raising your own brag. It may feel funny at first, and you may be bombarded by the kookie monster telling you not to root for yourself, but we encourage you to stick with it—to give it a fair chance, to give yourself a fair chance. We invite you to root, toot-toot your own horn.

Here is a good way to do it: the next time someone appreciates you with a compliment, take it in (rather than fending it off or denying it), and say something like:

"How perceptive of you to notice!"

"Could you repeat that three times?"

"And that's only one of my many strengths!"

"I sure am a wonderful person!"

"You're certainly fortunate to know me!"

We hope this action-project a-peals to you. Don't be surprised if it evokes peals of laughter from you—keep them coming. You can laugh all the way to the bank of self-esteem. Open up your humorous and playful savings account today. It will bring your self-esteem a great deal of interest.

❑ Activity #180: Plus Sign

This exercise is a new sign of the times. In fact, we encourage you to use the plus sign three times: the next time someone presents an idea (e.g., in a meeting, in a classroom, at a party) to you, try to think of three things you *like* about the idea *before* you allow yourself to think (or verbalize) anything negative. Again, while this may seem like such a simple idea, it is one that can be very difficult to implement—no thanks to ingrained killer phrases.

Or, try this one on for size—the next time you think of an idea, generate three things you like about it before you allow yourself to kill it. This action-project is good practice for those individuals who would like to maintain a positive outlook, as well as to communicate that outlook to others. It is a way of looking out for each other—sharing plusses can keep you from becoming nonplussed.

❑ Activity #181: World Book of Records

Another way of increasing your sense of agency (and humor and self-esteem) is to set a record. Get a copy of *Guinness World Records*. Then, look through it and pick a record you (and/or others) would like to challenge. You could also create your own challenge. Then, go ahead and try to break the record. At the very least, it should be a novel experience. Furthermore, if you are very successful, someone may even write a novel about your experience.

❑ Activity #182: Fametags

One way of helping people to focus on the positive is to turn nametags into fametags. Take a 5 x 8 card and print your name in big letters on it. For each letter in your name, identify at least one positive adjective that reflects an ability or quality you possess for which you are "famous"—the ones that people will remember you by. Be sure to allow yourself the "luxury" of bragging. After completing your card, take some time to mill around with others. Feel free to "tag" each other with additional positive adjectives.

❑ Activity #183: Ten You're

If you have tenure, then you have job security. If you receive "ten you're," then you will be more secure with yourself. Here is how this ritual works. E—each week, someone from your group is designated as "person of the week" (or "camper of the week," or "student of the day," etc.). Place a sheet of paper in a prominent place, with a picture of the "person of the week" on it. Head the paper with a title like "Ten Things You're Good At" or "Ten Things We Like About You." During the week, anyone can sign up an appreciation at any time. Of course, the end result is that the person takes away from this ten commanding reminders of her lovability and capability. You and your group will probably want to come back for "seconds" on this nourishing course of action.

❑ Activity #184: Construction Paper

A popular myth in our culture is that people grow best through constructive criticism. Actually, "constructive criticism" is just a euphemism for negative feedback. It is our culture's way of legitimizing killer phrases. We would much prefer to build on people's strengths and successes, rather than to focus on their "weaknesses."

This ritual invites you to carry out the "ten you're" idea on a daily basis with everyone, simultaneously. In this case, everyone puts up a sheet of "construction" paper with her name (or picture) on it. Anyone can place a validation on anyone else's sheet at any time. You may also want to structure in some time, specifically to work with the "construction" paper.

There are numerous variations of this activity. Some teachers, camp leaders, and parents we know have set up "validation envelopes" and "nice things boxes" for people to exchange appreciations. Others have set up a postal system for delivery of "positive" letters among people. Another idea is to create bulletin boards with such themes as: "I'm proud to be me …" and "I like the way you …"

❑ Activity #185: Pro Book

We are all probably familiar (too familiar) with celebrity roasts, as well as the age-old slam book—the book that is passed around from person to person—with each one writing disparaging remarks about the individual(s) being "slammed." Unfortunately, this can take place at lightning speed these days with anonymous postings in social media and on the web. How simple it would be to turn this into a pro-cedure, one in which only "pro" remarks would be made about a person. And what a surprise it would be to present the entire book to the person as a self-esteem present. Do you like our pro-posal?

❑ Activity #186: You Are a Natural Resource

We may not always see ourselves as "experts," but we certainly do have a lot of expertise. It is a crime to waste the resources within us. This activity is a way to help yourself and others to tap these natural resources. Hang up a shingle and set yourself up as a consultant on a particular topic or area. You can "learn as you go"—teaching others is one of the best ways of learning for yourself.

In order to help students increase their sense of competence, one teacher we know asked her students to set up a placard on their desks, announcing an area or skill that they saw as an area of expertise—one on which they would be willing to serve as a consultant to other students. Of course, a student was free to change the placard at any time.

This structure led to many beautiful "each one, teach one" situations. Not only did it help students to feel more competent, it also had the fringe benefit of encouraging cooperation and peer teaching in such areas as math skills, writing skills, reading, athletic skills, and drawing horse heads. Yes, drawing horse heads—each student was able to carve out her own bailiwick.

❑ Activity #187: Friendship Circles

Meals can be wonderful occasions for nourishment—physical, emotional, spiritual. You may eat as many as 75,000 meals in your life. That's a lot of opportunities for "food for thought." Friendship circles can "serve" a number of purposes, for example, enhancing self-esteem and developing a sense of community.

There are several ways you can set the stage—and set the table—for your friendship circle. Some people start each meal by joining hands and taking a moment of silence. Others will have someone share a poem, song, or thought that is important to her. Another option would be to have a "theme" of the meal (perhaps one of the "You Asked for It" questions in Activity #172), which everyone could address.

What other ideas can you cook up for friendship circles, for making meals meaning-full experiences (as opposed to eat-and-runs)? What courses do you want to prepare as a self-esteem gourmet? Wouldn't it be nice if every meal—all 75,000 of 'em—could be a testimonial dinner/lunch/breakfast—a testimonial to you and those sharing your table?

❑ Activity #188: Weekly Pro-Action Sheet

One of the strategies from the field of values clarification is called "the weekly reaction sheet." This strategy invites people to inventory their values, as they reflect on the previous week. In that regard, we would like to present a complementary ritual—the weekly pro-action sheet.

The weekly pro-action sheet gives you an opportunity to inventory the positive actions that you took in the past week and to set goals for positive behaviors in the upcoming week. We posit that it would be a positive experience for you to share what you have written with others. You may also be able to draw some interesting conclusions by looking for patterns in your sheets every month. Sometimes, you can "make a difference" by identifying similarities.

We encourage you to create your own weekly pro-action sheet. You might want to respond to and springboard off the following kinds of items:
- Ten things I did last week that I feel good about …
- Three people who helped me feel more lovable …
- Three people who helped me feel more capable …
- Three people I helped to feel more lovable …
- Three people I helped to feel more capable …
- What others did to help me feel more lovable/capable …
- What I did to help others feel more lovable/capable …
- The high point of the week for me …

- My autobiography for the past week …
- One thing I would like to work on/get better at …
- A success/achievement/accomplishment for me in the past week …
- In the past week, if I had received a telegram that would have made me feel really good, who would it have been from and what would it have said …
- If I had an Aladdin's lamp last week and could have made three wishes …
- Two ways I celebrated last week …
- One value I acted on in the past week …
- One value I would like to act on in the next week …
- In the past week, I was like a (metaphor) because …
- Last week, I wondered …
- Last week, I felt confident when …
- Last week, I felt competent when …
- Last week, I felt close to people when …
- If I had the last week "off" (with no responsibility), I would have …
- One way I interrupted a killer phrase …
- I have a dream …

❏ Activity #189: Comfort and Caring

Every single meeting, class, or workshop that we facilitate begins with "comfort and caring." This endeavor is a structured time set aside to deal with questions related to the comfort and caring of group members. People may raise questions ranging from "Where are the bathrooms?" to "When will we begin eating lunch?" to "Can somebody give me a ride home after the meeting" to "Can I stay at someone's home after the workshop session today?"

Comfort and caring is a vital ritual. Without it, we run the risk of having people stuck at the bottom of Maslow's need hierarchy—so concerned with physical and security issues that they do not have the attention to learn and grow and share with others. Comfort and caring is free—it frees people up to participate actively and to move toward what Maslow calls "self-actualization."

❏ Activity #190: Validation Circles

This activity is an opportunity for you to add-lib: *add*ing to your self-esteem can be a *lib*erating experience. Have the people in your group (e.g., class, camp cabin, family, office) form a circle. Each person, in turn (who wants a turn—the "pass" option is always available in this instance), gives a validation (to self or others) in 25 words or less. There are no comments or discussion.

The validation circle is a moving experience—it moves quickly from one person to the next. You may choose either to leave the validations open-ended, or to provide people with more structured (e.g., complete "I am proud that I ..." "One thing I appreciate about _____ is ..." etc.).

With younger children, we sometimes find it helpful to introduce this ritual by suggesting that they are "leaning" in the right direction for this exercise if they:
- <u>L</u>isten exquisitely well.
- <u>E</u>ach one who wants a turn can have one (also the right to pass).
- <u>A</u>ccept what others say (defer discussion).
- <u>N</u>o killer phrases or kookie monsters allowed on the premises.

After everyone has had a turn, you may find it helpful to have someone in the group sum up the sharing. Doing so can reinforce the listening norm.

❏ Activity #191: Do Your Own Think

We sometimes call this ritual "status quotations," because we place much status in using quotations as thought-provokers, feeling-provokers, and action-provokers. You might like to set up a "quotes wall" in the room, and encourage participants to create a quotes quilt relating to self-esteem. You will definitely want to check out Chapter 10 in our companion book, *Humanizing Outdoor and Environmental Education*: "Can I Quote You on That?: Quenching Quest for Quintessential Quotable Quotations" for dozens of quotes to jump-start your thinking.

You might choose to start your quilt by drawing from the quotes interwoven throughout this book. Or, the quotes that follow (some of which list the author, some have an unknown creator) may give you some mind food. Of course, we encourage you to "do your own think"—to think up your own quotes and add them to the quilt.

- To try and fail is at least to learn; to fail to try is to suffer the inestimable loss of what might have been. (Chester Barnard)
- Just as we can throttle our imagination, we can likewise accelerate it. (Alex Osborn)
- An oak is a nut that held its ground.
- Behold the turtle—she only makes progress when she sticks her neck out.
- Failure is the line of least persistence. (Alfred Brandt)
- The best place to find a helping hand is at the end of your arm.
- In the light of the influence of the self-concept on academic achievement, it would seem like a good idea for schools to follow the precept I saw printed on an automobile drag-strip racing program: "Every effort is made to ensure that each entry has a reasonable chance of victory." (William Purkey)
- Luck is the residue of design. (Branch Rickey)
- The surest way to corrupt a youth is to instruct him to hold in higher esteem those who think alike than those who think differently. (Nietzsche)
- People are like teabags—they don't know their own strength until they get in hot water.
- There are no errors when the game isn't played—but also no hits or runs either.

- Fear will make people do great things. Love allows them to do the impossible.
- There are no strangers in the world—only friends you have yet to meet.
- Wishing doesn't make it happen, but it won't happen if you don't wish.
- It takes 13 muscles to smile, 54 muscles to frown. (Joel Goodman)
- You'd better not compromise yourself—it's all you got. (Janis Joplin)
- He who's not busy being born, is busy dying. (Bob Dylan)
- I have never met a man who has given me as much trouble as myself. (D. L. Moody)
- In a mirror, everyone sees her best friend.
- Human beings can alter their lives by altering their attitudes of mind. (William James)

❏ Activity #192: Inverse Paranoid Projects

These unique and enjoyable action-projects aim to create more of what Jack Canfield calls "inverse paranoids"—people who think the world is out to do them good. By creating some positive self-fulfilling prophecies, we can aid people in developing seed-planting activities you could undertake:
- Verbally validate (appreciate) five or more people in your school, camp, or program.
- Plan a meal for someone new (to your school, camp, or program).
- Find in your wallet one symbol of a "success" you've had and see what others have found in their wallets.
- Clip out or draw a cartoon that you think will make someone laugh and give it or send it to that person.
- Send a special greeting card to someone who might not expect one from you.
- Write a letter to the local newspaper (or school or camp paper), commending somebody for doing something good.
- Do something nice for someone and keep it a secret.
- The next time someone brings up a new idea in a discussion, try to say "yes, and…," rather than "yes, but …"
- Sing or play a recording of your favorite song to someone.
- On the turnpike, pay the toll for the car in back of you.
- Send someone an anonymous positive note.
- Say hello to ten strangers in one day.
- Help carry packages at the grocery store—for free.
- Throw a surprise "unbirthday" party for someone you know.
- Make one positive phone call per day.
- Say "thank you" five times each day.
- During a conversation with someone else, say "to be perfectly honest with you …" and complete the sentence with something positive rather than negative.
- Have participants in your program lead activities that the staff would sign up to take.

- Bring in a favorite possession and keep it around for the year.
- Ask each participant to bring an article from the newspaper that contains some good news.
- Make a recording of everyone's individual contribution to the rest of the group and then play it for them.
- Have a special "good deeds" day in which the participants do helpful things for others.
- Create 25 more "inverse paranoid projects" and carry them out.

❏ Activity #193: Plant Postures

Go outside and locate shrubs, trees, and other plants that remind you of how you hold your body, when you feel good about yourself. Then find plants that remind you of how you hold your body, when you don't feel so good about yourself. Can you tell when other people are not feeling very good about themselves by how they hold and move their bodies? What internal sentences work best for you to help you feel better about yourself?

❏ Activity #: 194: Power Phrases and Poems

Think about how you put yourself down. For example, do you sometimes think you are too heavy, small, slow, shy, or clumsy? When you find something that you do to sabotage yourself, look around outside to find a clue that will help you combat that negative message. Find examples of strength, beauty, skill, or other strengths in the natural world. Write power phrases for each example and repeat them slowly out loud or to yourself. Does repeating a power phrase help you feel better about yourself? Maybe, you could say it again when you are feeling low. Some examples of power phases from nature include the following:
- I am a flower bud, bursting open with beauty.
- I am a solid mountain peak, lifted above the clouds.
- Like a caterpillar, I eat away my problems bite by bite.

   You may want to try rhyming words and write power poems:
- Like a stream, I am supreme
- Like a tree, I can be me.
- Like a beautiful bird, I will be heard.

❏ Activity #195: Creative License

Go outside with a partner and create a new nature and human nature activity that helps you feel better about yourself. After a few minutes, come back and share your activity with the group. Did doing this with a partner make it easier to create a new activity?

❏ Activity #196: Nature's Word Mirrors

Create a nature mirror by writing metaphors and similes about objects and events you find around you. Write metaphors and similes that highlight nature's beauty, attractiveness, and strengths. A metaphor is a direct comparison of two things: "Clouds are soft pillows." Similes are comparisons using the words, "like" or "as." For example, "trees are like proud soldiers standing at attention." The substitute the words "I am" for each object or event and read them aloud. How did you feel when you substituted the words, "I am"?

❑ Activity #197: Priceless Art

Go outside and create an art form that shows something good about yourself (a personal strength or talent), using some of the things you find in nature, such as clay, plant color pigments on sandpaper, rocks, acorns, sticks, or leaf collages. What are some of the inner messages you told yourself while you were creating this art? Do you repeat these messages in other situations?

❑ Activity #198: New Growth Search

Look for three examples of new growth on the tips of three different kinds of trees and shrubs. Measure these lengths of new growth and think of ways that you have shown new growth in your life. Match these ways with the different lengths of plant growth. For example, match the greatest growth with how you grew most and the shortest growth with how you grew least. Do you create situations for new growth or wait for them to happen? What can you do today to promote some new personal growth?

❑ Activity #199: Strength Feathers

Dumbo, the big-eared Disney elephant, thought that he could fly because of a magic feather he held in his trunk. When he accidentally dropped the feather, he found out that he could still fly without it. The feather helped him take a risk and believe in himself. Find an object outside that will help you take a risk to do something that you want to be better at doing. How are natural symbols helpful in building confidence? How do symbols help to give confidence and strength? Did you learn anything about yourself by doing this activity?

❑ Activity #200: Nature's Gifts to Yourself

Spend several minutes by yourself in a natural area. Decide what kind of gift from your area you can give to yourself and then receive it. (Caution: Don't do anything dangerous or destroy other living things.) Consider giving yourself:

• Beautiful cloud shapes
• Pleasant smells
• Natural sounds
• A favorite rock
• A rest in the grass
• A tree hug
• A special stick

Was it easy or hard to decide on a gift to give yourself? Is this true for you when receiving other gifts, like compliments or praise? When you are feeling low, what natural gift can you give yourself?

❑ Activity #201: Left-Handed Complements

When it comes time to say "goodbye" to people with whom you are close (e.g., when camp ends for the summer, when the school year comes to a close, when a visit from friends or relatives is over), you may want to find a ritual that brings closure and that brings you closer to the people.

We have to hand it to you … our left-hand, that is. One light and lively way of saying goodbye is to extend to each other left-handed complements. Unlike left-handed compliments (which leave kookie monster crumbs all over you), left-handed complements leave you feeling more complete.

If you gotta go, you gotta go. It's better to go feeling complete. So, extend yourself and your left hand. While you are shaking hands left-handed, share an appreciation/validation with the other person that will leave that person feeling more complete. Shaking hands left-handed may lead you to shake with laughter. It can be fun to do things differently. As such, it can play an important part in adding lightness to departures.

"I always wanted to be somebody, but now I realize I should have been more specific."

—Lily Tomlin

GIVING CREDIT WHERE CREDIT IS DUE

We salute Jack Canfield and William Purkey as two of the pioneers in focusing on the importance of self-concept. See the extensive Resources chapter in our companion book, *Humanizing Outdoor and Environmental Education*, for annotations on *100 Ways to Enhance Self-Concept in the Classroom* (by Jack Canfield and Harold Wells) and *Self Concept and School Achievement* (by William Purkey).

Check Chapters 5, 7, 8, and 9 in our companion book, *Humanizing Outdoor and Environmental Education*, which is described on pages 168-169 in Chapter 8 of the book you are holding. You'll find loads of additional practical activities and insights on developing self-esteem.

CHAPTER 7

CARTOONS TO LEAVE YOU LAUGHING … AND THINKING ABOUT NATURE AND HUMAN NATURE

Chad was oblivious to the fact that he had a very large carbon footprint.

"There is a growing acceptance of the importance of cartoons: they capture the unofficial values and attitudes of the time, providing a street level view of the world."

—Ian F. Grant

With inflation, a picture is now worth much more than a thousand words. John McPherson's very popular *Close to Home* cartoon reaches over 40 million people a day throughout the world. In this chapter, John reaches out to you with a light yet serious look at camps, nature, and human nature.

With many serious environmental issues facing us, John shows that a sense of humor can help us move from "grim and bear it" to "grin and share it." As he holds up a mirror to our reality, hopefully, we can laugh at ourselves in the reflection, which will help us to move on and take action to protect and preserve our planet. As our world gets proverbially smaller all the time, we need humor to build bridges (not walls) between countries and cultures. It is important to remember that on this planet, the reality is that "we're all in it together." As Erma Bombeck once said, "When humor goes, there goes civilization." In order to take on the challenge of providing TLC to Mother Nature, we need to nurture our sense of humor.

With tongue protruding at least slightly in cheek, John sheds some light (and lightness) on camps and youth sports:

CLOSE TO HOME © 2001 John McPherson. Reprinted with permission of Andrews McMeel Syndication. All rights reserved.

CLOSE TO HOME © 1994 John McPherson. Reprinted with permission of Andrews McMeel Syndication. All rights reserved.

CLOSE TO HOME © 2006 John McPherson. Reprinted with permission of Andrews McMeel Syndication. All rights reserved.

A veteran camper, Randy knew it was critical to play dead if he should encounter a bear.

John goes on to enlighten and lighten heavy issues like pollution, carbon footprints, and global warming:

"Today I'd like to discuss global warming and its effect on ocean levels."

"This global warming stuff is getting out of hand."

"I'd chalk it up to just another crazy backyard hobby, except that he's the world's leading authority on global warming."

John is a master at bringing together HAHA (humor) and AHA (creativity) in these cartoons that invite you to think (and laugh) outside the box when it comes to generating alternative forms of green energy (who knows… some of these Rube Goldberg ideas and contraptions might work):

Concerned about soaring energy costs, Connie embarks on her biggest craft project ever and knits a wool sweater for their house.

CLOSE TO HOME © 2005 John McPherson. Reprinted with permission of Andrews McMeel Syndication. All rights reserved.

CLOSE TO HOME © 2006 John McPherson. Reprinted with permission of Andrews McMeel Syndication. All rights reserved.

A dramatic breakthrough in the world of alternative energy: canine tail power.

"We've found a way to harness the energy of kids' thumb motions when they are texting!"

This chapter has offered just a small taste of John McPherson's many thousands of cartoons. John's perspective-giving cartoons and creativity are brilliant in tapping and putting into practice the positive power of humor. To wit:

- "From there to here, from here to there, funny things are everywhere." (Dr. Seuss)
- "Life is a tragedy, when seen in close-up, but a comedy in longshot." (Charlie Chaplin)
- "Two things reduce prejudice: education and laughter." (Laurence J. Peter)
- "Life is too important to be taken seriously." (Oscar Wilde)
- "Good humor is a philosophical state of mind. It seems to say to Nature that we take her no more seriously than She takes us." (M. Dale Baughman)
- "An optimist laughs to forget; a pessimist forgets to laugh." (Tom Nansbury)
- "To be playful and serious at the same time is possible, and it defines the ideal mental condition." (John Dewey)
- Humor is not a trick, not jokes. Humor is a presence in the world—like grace—and shines on everybody. (Garrison Keillor)

John McPherson's *Close to Home* cartoons are a real presence in the world and a present to the world. His humor and creativity shine on everybody.

"A good cartoon can convey, at a glance, a wealth of information; it can epitomize an idea better than a thousand words; it is remembered when words are forgotten; it is instant enlightenment."

—Sir John Marshall

GIVING CREDIT WHERE CREDIT IS DUE

John McPherson's humor and creativity shine on everybody through his internationally syndicated *Close to Home* cartoons and through his laughter-and-applause-generating public speaking. Be sure to see more information on John's cartoons and his presentations at the end of the next chapter of this book.

The eight humor-related quotes at the end of this chapter and a number of other quotes sprinkled throughout our two books are drawn from Joel Goodman's book, *Laffirmations: 1,001 Ways to Add Humor to Your Life and Work*. This book is annotated in the next chapter and is available through The HUMOR Project's HUMOResources online bookstore: https://www.humorproject.com/humoresources/productdetail.php?product=101.

CHAPTER 8
RESOURCES: WHERE DO YOU GO FROM HERE?

Andersen Ross/Blend Images/Thinkstock

"Reading one book is like eating one potato chip."

—Diane Duane

By reading this book, you have just eaten one potato chip. Bet you can't eat just one. In fact, our companion book, *Humanizing Outdoor and Environmental Education*, is filled with a lot of food-for-thought and would be a real treat for you to consume next.

Knapp, Clifford E. & Goodman, Joel (2017). *Humanizing Outdoor and Environmental Education*. Monterey, California: Healthy Learning.

This companion book provides the foundation for the book you currently hold in your hands. It is a thought-full and mindful guide to the humanistic approach to outdoor and environmental education. This volume focuses on the "why's" for planning and implementing nature experiences for people of all ages. In addition to a chapter on curriculum and program development for schools and camps, this volume draws on the expertise, experience, and wisdom of trend-setting pioneers and practitioners like Cheryl Charles, Richard Louv, Joseph Cornell, Roger Greenaway, Jeff McKay, Matt Weinstein, and Pamela Kekich.

The book includes probing, intriguing, informative, insightful, and inspiring interviews with them on the "new nature movement," nature mindfulness and awareness, reflecting and reviewing experiential learning, cooperative play, adventure learning, humanistic camps, and creative coaching. The chapters are filled with tips and practical activities that invite active and interactive learning. The book also provides a detailed case study of the leading-edge Human Relations Youth Adventure Camp and offers an extensive chapter with over 125 annotations for books, periodicals, websites, and organizations in the humanistic, outdoor, and environmental education fields. As a bonus, this book includes thought-provoking quotes to jump-start your brain and heart about the connection between nature and human nature.

Available from Healthy Learning at www.healthylearning.com.

JOEL'S NOTES AND CLIFF'S NOTES

As noted previously, our companion book, *Humanizing Outdoor and Environmental Education*, offers a wide-ranging, rich Resources chapter. We strongly encourage you to tap that terrific trove. In the meantime, the following is a sampling of the timeless books that we have written in the past that provide part of the foundation for *Humanizing Outdoor and Environmental Education* and *201 Nature and Human Nature Activities*. Also included is information on cartoonist John McPherson, whom you just experienced in the last chapter, as well as material on the impactful pioneering work of Joel's The HUMOR Project.

BOOKS BY JOEL AND CLIFF

❑ Goodman, Joel. (1995). *Laffirmations: 1,001 ways to add humor to your life and work*. Deerfield Beach, FL: Health Communications, Inc.

Joel believes that ""Seven days without laughter make one weak."" With this in mind, he delivers 52 weeks of ideas on how to increase your H.Q. (Humor Quotient). Each day of the year includes a thought-provoking quote (some of which appear in this book), along with action-inviting, practical humor tips to help you get more smileage out of your life and work. With this timely and timeless book, you will be grinning from year to year! Available through HUMOResources online bookstore at https://www.humorproject.com/humoresources/productdetail.php?product=101.

❑ Goodman, Joel (editor). (1978). *Turning points: New developments, new directions in values clarification, volume I*. Saratoga Springs, NY: Creative Resources Press.

This book contains a stimulating and varied collection of 20 articles by leaders in the field who explore the very latest thinking on values clarification theory and practice. This volume explores the applications of values clarification to education, families, business, youth organizations, and trainers/consultants. It also contains sections on new practical strategies, questions and answers about values clarification, and annotated resource lists.

❏ _____. (1979). *Turning points: New developments, new directions in values clarification, volume II.* Saratoga Springs, NY: Creative Resources Press.

There were so many good contributions to the first volume that a second volume was published in response to popular demand. Like Volume I, this book has sections on innovations in theory and practice, new strategies, and resources in the field. It includes descriptions of how to apply the values clarification approach to a wide variety of fields and helping professionals.

❏ Goodman, Joel & Furman, Irv. *Magic and the educated rabbit: A handbook for teachers, parents, and helping professionals.* Paoli, PA: Instructo/McGraw-Hill, 1981.

This book features a collection of easy-to-do and powerful magic tricks. What is unique about this book is that the authors describe hundreds of ways of using the tricks to address important learning objectives (e.g., using magic as an aid to learning subject matter, creating a positive learning environment, helping young people learn such life skills as observing, communicating, enhancing self-esteem, etc.).

❏ Goodman, Joel & Huggins, Ken. *Let the buyer be aware: A practical handbook for consumers, teachers, and parents.* La Mesa, CA: The Wright Group, 1981.

This involving book includes hundreds of practical activities and ideas for: taking charge of your lifestyle; making sense of important consumer issues; developing life skills; helping students to become more effective consumers and citizens; and applying the values clarification approach to consumer education. The authors also provide a powerful curriculum-development model, which teachers and parents can use to generate millions of ideas for classroom lessons and family discussions.

❏ Knapp, Clifford E. (1988). *Creating humane climates outdoors: A people skills primer.* Charleston, WV: ERIC Clearinghouse on Rural Education and Small Schools and Appalachia Educational Laboratory.

Suggestions and activities for creating humane climate outdoors, including building intentional communities, teaching intrapersonal skills (becoming aware of feelings; affirming personal worth; demonstrating humor and imagination; recognizing personal power; and others), and interpersonal skills (communicating thoughts/feeling; empathizing; interpreting nonverbal language; questioning; validating others; and others). Annotated bibliography and interview with Sue Flory, former Human Relations Youth Adventure Camp director, included.

❏ _____. (1992). *Lasting lessons: A teacher's guide to reflecting on experience.* Charleston, WV: ERIC Clearinghouse on Rural Education and Small Schools and Appalachia Educational Laboratory.

One of the early books for experiential educators, designed to help with skills of reflecting/reviewing. Covers educational theory, practical leadership issues, questioning techniques, and alternative strategies to facilitate groups. Still available on the Internet.

❑ _____. (1996). *Just beyond the classroom: Community adventures for interdisciplinary learning*. Charleston, WV: ERIC Clearinghouse on Rural Education and Small Schools.

This book contains background of educational reforms through outdoor education, planning for out-of-school lessons, and outlines for 12 outdoor adventure themes. Eight appendices provide additional aids for implementing lessons. Many activities can be taught in the city, as well as in rural areas.

❑ _____. (1999). *In accord with nature*. Charleston, WV: ERIC Clearinghouse on Rural Education and Small Schools and Appalachia Educational Laboratory.

The subtitle, "helping students form an environmental ethic using outdoor experience and reflection," describes the purpose of the book. Filled with many ideas for conducting lessons about the threatened quality of the environment. Values and ethics resources and a bibliography direct the reader to other places for assistance.

❑ Knapp, Clifford E. & Goodman, Joel. (1981). *Humanizing environmental education: A guide for leading nature and human nature activities*. Martinsville, IN: American Camping Association.

This book is the original classic that has now been revised and expanded in 2017 into two books: *Humanizing Outdoor and Environmental Education and 201 Nature and Human Nature Activities* (the book you are now holding).

❑ Knapp, Clifford E. & Smith, Thomas E. (Eds.). (2005). *Exploring the power of solo, silence, and solitude*. Boulder, CO: Association for Experiential Education.

A compilation of 22 chapters from an eclectic group of university educators, clergy, and experiential education consultants and instructors divided into four parts: theoretical frameworks, research results, leadership in action, and personal perspectives. Appendices include a dialogue with the editors, quotations about the solo experience, activities for those on solos, and an epilogue.

❑ Read, Donald, Simon, Sidney, & Goodman, Joel. (1977). *Health education: The search for values*. Englewood Cliffs: Prentice Hall.

This book presents new developments in how the values clarification approach is defined, along with new applications to the field of health education. The authors present dozens of practical activities focusing on such content areas as human sexuality, drug abuse, and nutrition, while simultaneously showing how these exercises can be used to develop valuing skills. The book includes an innovative chapter on humanistic approaches to evaluation.

❏ Smith, Thomas E. & Knapp, Clifford E. (Eds.). (2011). *Sourcebook of experiential education: Key thinkers and their contributions.* New York/London: Routledge Taylor & Francis Group.

The book has four parts that cover educational philosophers/theorists; nature study, outdoor and environmental education; psychologists/sociologists; and school/program founders. Readers learn about who influenced today's leaders of experiential nature and human nature programs and curricula.

❏ Weinstein, Matt & Goodman, Joel. *Playfair: Everybody's guide to noncompetitive play.* (1980). San Luis Obispo, CA: Impact Publishers.

The classic in the field of cooperative play. It includes a lively look at why we should be serious about play, along with 60 fun, highly participatory games, exercises, and icebreakers used around the world that invite cooperation, inclusion, and self-esteem. The activities are designed to build people up and bring people together in schools, camps, colleges, conferences, families, meetings, and corporate events. The book features unique and insightful chapters on how to lead and facilitate playful experiences and how you can create a million of your own positive, noncompetitive activities.

> *"Outside of a dog, a book is man's best friend.*
> *Inside a dog, it's too dark to read."*
>
> —Groucho Marx

OTHER RESOURCES AND SERVICES

❏ The HUMOR Project, Inc.

Founded by Dr. Joel Goodman in 1977, The HUMOR Project is the first organization in the world to focus full-time on the positive power of humor and creativity. Its speakers bureau has presented keynote speeches, seminars, and workshops for schools, hospitals, business corporations, camps, human service agencies, associations, and conventions for more than three million people in all 50 states and on all seven continents. It operates the HUMOResources online bookstore and has sponsored 55 international humor conferences that have featured and honored laughter luminaries like Steve Allen, Sid Caesar, Victor Borge, Jay Leno, Carol Channing, Bob Newhart, Art Buchwald, Gilda Radner, David Hyde Pierce, Lucie Arnaz, the Smothers Brothers, etc. Visit www.HumorProject.com for more on this fun-of-a-kind organization. Email info@ HumorProject.com to sign up for their free bi-monthly *Laughing Matters* e-zine that contains humor tips, quotes, cartoons, anecdotes, and the latest in the humor field. The e-zine is designed for anyone who believes in humoristic education and wants to tap the positive power of humor in everyday life and work (put "Humanizing/Humorizing" in the subject line).

❑ *Close to Home*

In the previous chapter, you had a chance to enjoy and experience *Close to Home*, which is John McPherson's syndicated cartoon that appears in 700+ newspapers worldwide. John not only has published over 20 book collections of his cartoons, he also has an award-winning line of greeting cards, a yearly block calendar, and numerous other licensed products. John is part of The HUMOR Project's speakers bureau and been an active speaker for organizations, schools, associations, hospitals, and human service agencies around the country. To contact John about speaking, email info@ HumorProject.com. To get a taste every day for more of his cartoons that will invite you to laugh and think, visit http://www.gocomics.com/closetohome.

ABOUT THE AUTHORS

Dr. Joel Goodman, director of The HUMOR Project in Saratoga Springs, New York, is a popular speaker and workshop leader whose programs on humanistic and experiential education and the positive power of humor and creativity have touched and tickled the lives of millions. In fact, Joel is one of only two professional speakers in the world to have presented in all 50 states and on all seven continents. Since 1968, he has spoken at national and state conferences and at in-house training programs for schools, human service organizations, corporations, non-profits, government agencies, and professional associations.

After receiving his B.A. from the University of Pennsylvania and his M.Ed and Ed.D. from the University of Massachusetts in Amherst, Joel served as the associate director of the Maryland Leadership Workshops and the National Humanistic Education Center. He founded The HUMOR Project in 1977 as the first organization in the world to focus full-time on the positive power of humor and creativity.

Author of hundreds of articles, columns, and magazines, Joel has written/co-authored 10 books, including *Laffirmations: 1,001 Ways to Add Humor to Your Life and Work; Playfair: Everybody's Guide to Noncompetitive Play; Health Education: The Search for Values; Turning Points: New Developments, New Directions in Values Clarification;* and *Magic and the Educated Rabbit*. Joel has also created the unique www.HumorProject.com website and publishes the free *Laughing Matters* e-zine.

Described by *New Age* magazine as "the first full-time humor educator in the world," Joel's pioneering work has been featured in 7000-plus TV and radio shows, newspapers, and magazines in 175+ countries, including: *The TODAY Show*, PBS, ABC NEWS' prime-time special on *The Mystery of Happiness*, BBC, *Latenight America, Donahue, All Things Considered*, the front page of *The Wall Street Journal, The New York Times Sunday Magazine, The Washington Post, USA Today, Readers' Digest, Successful Meetings*, numerous Associated Press national features, and *The Daily Show with Jon Stewart*.

In 1995, Joel was delighted to join Red Skelton, Willard Scott, and Meadowlark Lemon in receiving the prestigious International Lifetime of Laughter Achievement Award. He is the founder of AHA! (American Humor Association), which includes 165,000 people interested in the positive power of humor. Believing that it is important to "do well and do good" at the same time, The HUMOR Project has provided grants to 500 schools, hospitals, and human service agencies to help them develop services and resources that tap the positive power of humor and creativity.

Joel takes his work seriously and himself lightly, while helping people to get more smileage out of their lives and jobs. His family is most precious to him: wife—Margie, children and their spouses—Adam and Hilda, Alyssa and Jake, and grandson—Jakobe. Joel has participated in sports all his life and loves convening with Mother Nature on his daily long walks with camera in hand.

You can contact Joel at Joel@HumorProject.com.

Dr. Cliff Knapp is a retired professor of education from the faculty of Outdoor Teacher Education at Northern Illinois University (NIU) in DeKalb, Illinois. His teaching career spanned all levels of education, including elementary, junior high, and high school, as well as 29 years of undergraduate and graduate-level instruction at Southern Illinois University (SIU) and NIU.

Cliff was introduced to the field of outdoor education in 1958 when he enrolled in a camping education course at Paterson State Teachers College in Wayne, New Jersey. He continued from there as a camp counselor, director, and co-founder of the Human Relations Youth Adventure Camp in New York's Adirondack Mountains. He received his bachelor's degree in 1961, his master's degree in 1963, and his doctorate in 1973.

Cliff taught science and was the director of resident outdoor education in Ridgewood, New Jersey for seven and one-half years. At several universities he taught courses in outdoor/environmental/place-based education, an undertaking that included curriculum and instruction, teaching methods, science, nature interpretation, environmental ethics, nature arts and crafts, and research.

He has led hundreds of workshops at professional conferences and meetings, such as the Association for Experiential Education, American Camp Association, North American Association for Environmental Education, and the National Wildlife Federation. His workshop topics include Projects WILD and Learning Tree, Leopold Education Project, Children's Nature Literature, Reflecting on Experience, Questioning Strategies, Finding Silence and Solitude, Environmental Ethics, Early Naturalists' Skills, Fire-Making, Native Uses of Bison, and Images of Nature.

Cliff has published widely in the fields of camping, outdoor, and environmental education. He has authored or co-authored 12 books, as well as over 150 book chapters and journal articles. He has written for journals, including *Science and Children, Green Teacher, Camping Magazine, Journal of Experiential Education, Nature Study,* and *Taproot.* His latest books include *Lasting Lessons* (1992); *In Accord with Nature* (1999); *Exploring the Power of Solo, Silence, and Solitude* (with Tom Smith) (2005); and *Sourcebook of Experiential Education* (with Tom Smith) (2011). In 2017, he had two companion books (with Joel Goodman) published by Healthy Learning that were updated and expanded from *Humanizing Environmental Education* (1981).

Cliff loves to read, write, teach, carve wooden birds, and walk outdoors. His passion is studying Native American cultures, including participating in sacred ceremonies and collecting indigenous arts and crafts. He teaches and serves on boards of directors for a rural school built in 1883 and a working gristmill first built in 1847. After more than 56 years as an outdoor teacher, he still enjoys sharing what he knows about nature and education. He lives with his wife, Nancy, in Oregon, Illinois. He has three grown daughters, Dawn, Eve, and Jenny.

You can contact Cliff at cknapp@niu.edu.